WE ARE THE MAJORITY!

THE LIFE *and* PASSIONS *of a* PATRIOT

MARK ROBINSON

REPUBLIC

BOOK PUBLISHERS

WE ARE THE MAJORITY!

FIRST EDITION

Copyright 2022 Mark Robinson

Hardcover ISBN: 9781645720515

Ebook ISBN: 9781645720522

For inquiries about volume orders, please contact:

Republic Book Publishers

27 West 2oth Street

Suite 1103

New York NY 10011

editor@republicbookpublishers.com

Published in the United States by Republic Book Publishers

Distributed by Independent Publishers Group

www.ipgbook.com

Book designed by Mark Karis

Cover photograph by AP Photo/Gerry Broome

Printed in the United States of America

There are two very important women in my life. I want to honor them both here.

That said, I dedicate this book to the memory of my mother, who taught me to have faith in God, to be a man, and to stand up and stand firm when being confronted.

I would also like to dedicate this book to my wife, Yolanda.

Yolanda, without you, I have no idea where I would be in this world. Marrying and starting a family with you returned me to the path my mom had taught me to walk. Before you came along, I was drifting through life without a purpose or goal. A wild streak had taken over me, and who knows what sort of trouble I may have found. I thank God for his grace in keeping me safe and leading me to you, the beautiful woman who would give me a reason to live responsibly and find direction. Yolanda, you and I are one, and while we may drive each other crazy at times, you always know what is right and help keep me straight along the way. You have always wanted the best for me, and I want the same for you. I love you.

CONTENTS

ACKNOWLEDGMENTS

THE JOURNEY that this book helps to explain would not have been possible without my family. They have supported me from day one. I did not have one family member say, "You shouldn't be doing that." My wife, my daughter, my son, my mother-in-law, and my sister-in-law have been 100 percent supportive in all of my efforts. Even though my sister-in-law and I do not see eye-to-eye on every political point, she is one of my biggest cheerleaders. I would not be able to do this without their unwavering support and belief in what I am doing.

My journey up to this point would not have been possible without the following people and organizations:

- North Carolina Sixth District Chair Lee Haywood, who was the first to reach out to me when this roller-coaster ride began. I came home to find his card in my door. Of all the people I have met in politics, Lee is a firebrand. He believes fervently in the Republican cause and conservative politics. Lee is a solid Christian man and one of my biggest supporters.

- NRA CEO Wayne LaPierre, who has been a great supporter from the very beginning.

- Former Director of NRA-ILA Chris Cox, who supported and embraced me even before he was sure of all my politics.

- The North Carolina GOP, an organization filled with many wonderful people who have been a driving force in this pursuit. Their belief in me has been a great encouragement.

- Grassroots North Carolina, a group that was present the night of the now-famous Greensboro City Council meeting. Two of their representatives were there, prepared to stand up to the leftist mass. Grassroots NC is responsible for sharing the video of the speech that put me on the radar.

- Congressman Mark Walker, who first contacted Fox News with the video. His support from the beginning has been instrumental.

Additionally, I want to acknowledge my social media friends and followers—the 15,000 followers I had before this all started and the thousands more who now follow me since the speech. Even if we disagree, it's only in an effort to find solutions to keep this republic strong. Thank you for sharing my message.

Finally, I want to acknowledge all of the law-abiding citizens of the United States of America. You are the majority, and I am you.

PROLOGUE

THE RIFLE

ONE DAY in 2018 as I was perusing my social networks, I saw a post from a friend of mine with a photo of his son shooting a rifle. It was an AR-15 type rifle, but with more bells and whistles than the standard model. By 2018 my kids were grown, and I finally had time to participate in a few personal activities that had fallen by the wayside while the children were growing up. Rifles have meant a lot to me in life. I was in the military for nearly seven years. Most importantly, I was on the JROTC rifle team in high school. JROTC in many ways changed my life in high school and greatly influenced the trajectory of the sort of young man I would become. So it would not have been a surprise to anyone who knew me that I was interested in obtaining a rifle similar to the one in my friend's photo. The problem was where exactly to find one with all those trimmings. I sent my friend a message asking where he got the rifle. His reply told me that he had essentially built it himself. He had bought a basic semiautomatic rifle and added the components to make it into the version he'd given his son. I asked some of my friends who were knowledgeable about guns, and they told me that even though

I could purchase a basic AR-15 type rifle at Walmart and modify it, I shouldn't go that route.

"No, no. You need to buy one at the gun show when it comes to town in Greensboro," one friend told me. "They'll have what you want—and for a good price."

I was excited. I started saving my money to go to a gun show and purchase a rifle for myself.

"Greensboro City Council to cancel annual gun show," I heard as I listened to the news one winter morning that same year. I was getting ready for work, but the alarm on my personal antenna immediately began to vibrate. I had been planning to buy a gun at this very show. Then my *political* antenna went active as I heard the reason behind the push to cancel the show.

On February 14, just weeks before, a disturbed young man had killed seventeen students at Marjory Stoneman Douglas High School in Parkland, Florida. He'd murdered them in a mass shooting with an AR-15 type rifle. Now the Greensboro City Council proposed that Greensboro cancel our upcoming gun show. They would do this as a "response" to the Parkland shootings.

I was upset. No, I was furious. What did the action of a depraved shooter three states away have to do with me wanting to buy a rifle? Nothing! I had by this time become a proud defender of our Constitution, including the Second Amendment, our right to bear arms. I was a law-abiding man who was looking forward to purchasing a rifle at a gun show. I drove to work that day frustrated as I thought about the leftist gun control narrative that had now come to my hometown. Of course I felt awful about the lives lost in Florida. But I felt I was being punished for the actions of a criminal.

I did what I often do these days. I made my feelings known with a post on social media. In the timeline of replies to my post, someone noted that the city council did not have the lawful authority to cancel the gun show; only the Greensboro Coliseum director could make that decision. I was relieved. I presumed that the gun show would go on as planned because the coliseum would not want to lose the money from hosting it.

But the city council would not let the matter go. By this time, the city attorney had made it clear that the city council could not cancel the show without expensive repercussions. They didn't seem to care and continued to push the issue. They decided to hold a meeting to discuss "gun violence." I heard about this meeting the same way I first heard about the gun show controversy—while watching the news before work. The meeting was to be held that very evening, at 5:30 p.m.

My frustration rose once again. I was familiar with anti-gun political rhetoric. I knew what was about to happen. The school shooting in Parkland, Florida, had given the left another talking point, another emotional means to use the violence perpetrated by criminals and the criminally insane to push for getting rid of all guns. I suspected that the meeting that evening would be packed, most likely by college-aged activists. I imagined them giving speeches about the fears of gun violence in their schools. I knew the whole point of the hearing was to sway the coliseum director to cancel our local gun show.

"You need to go to that meeting," I thought to myself.

I went to work, still thinking about the meeting. I talked to my coworkers about it. I told anyone who would listen what I thought was going to happen that evening.

"I need to get to that meeting," I kept saying to myself.

But I had to work till 4:30 p.m., and the 5:30 meeting would be packed. I wrestled in my spirit. I felt I needed to attend. Yet at the same time something inside was holding me back.

Was it fear that I felt? Was I scared to stand up for my beliefs?

I pondered the question, but finally I came to the inevitable conclusion: I would be a hypocrite if I did not attend. How could I stay away from a vital meeting in my own community and say I cared about gun rights? I had to represent my beliefs and stand with those who believe in the Second Amendment.

I continued to be preoccupied with the meeting during every free moment of my workday. If I went, what would I do? I could just attend, as a presence. Should I say anything? What would I say? I had no time to prepare a speech. But shouldn't I say *something*? Make a point, at least? What would make the most impact?

At one point when I thought aloud about my decision, a friend of mine said, "What does it matter? All you can do is talk. Those people are going to do whatever they want to do, and there's nothing you can change about it."

I knew there was a measure of truth in what he said. Talking might change nothing. He might have been right about the short term,, but he was wrong about the power of sticking to one's ideals and articulating the reasons why.

I looked at him and said, "Just talk? You know the American Revolution didn't start with that shot heard 'round the world. It started with talking, with someone asking, 'Why can't we be free?'"

I walked away from my friend and went straight to the restroom. I closed the door, looked at my reflection in the mirror. "You have to go to that meeting," I told myself. "You don't have to say anything, but you have to go stand in that room. You have to be counted as one of those who support that gun show. You need to go, Mark. Because there will be someone there speaking up for the right to hold that gun show, and you ought to be there to support them."

I took a long breath. It was settled. I was going to that meeting.

I left work, went home to quickly grab a bite to eat, told my wife where I was going and headed to the city council meeting.

I was nervous as I drove downtown. At this point, I was not a stranger to expressing myself on political matters. Yet this was different. I wasn't talking to my conservative friends or posting opinions online to those who already agreed with me. This wouldn't be sitting in the comfort of my home, typing political commentary from behind the safety of a screen. As I drove, I wondered just how fiery the meeting might get. I was sure there would be arguing, fighting with words like cats and dogs.

As I arrived, I took a seat among all the other citizens there. I listened to several people speak, all in support of gun control, most attempting to draw bogus connections between legal gun ownership and crime and violence and failing spectacularly. Someone would finish and I would think, "That is the stupidest thing that I've ever heard." Then that individual would sit down, and another person would speak, and I would think, "No, *that* is the stupidest thing I've ever heard." Then up popped another making a flawed, nonsensical argument ,and I thought, "No, this must be some type of stupid contest because now *that's* the stupidest thing that I've ever heard."

This meeting was supposed to discuss gun violence in relation to whether the city ought to host a gun show, but people kept saying things that had nothing to do with the subject. No one had given a good reason why the show shouldn't take place, or why thousands of peoples' rights should be infringed.

There was a lot of talk about this minority, and that minority, and this cause, and that cause. But nothing addressed the rights of the huge majority of law-abiding citizens in our city. Then, a young man stood up in front of the whole city council, in front of all those cameras and people, to give his speech.

Right in the middle of his speech he blurted out, "We all know that men who have big Glocks have . . . small brains."

There it was. The ultimate stupidity. And it was a vulgar stupidity at that. He had just made a quasi-dirty joke right in the middle of a serious city council meeting discussing important issues for American citizens. I looked over at the council members, expecting them to at least suggest he tone it down. No one said anything.

This was turning into a clown show.

My frustration rose to a new level. I turned in my chair and let out an audible sigh of disgust. The young woman next to me glanced at me. I suspect she was wondering, "What is wrong with this man?"

I thought to myself, "I don't care if I have to push the guards out of the way, I am going to say something." I got up and stormed toward the man in charge of the order of speakers. I asked him if it was too late to sign up to speak. He said that it was not. So I signed up. The courier carried it up to the mayor and I went to get in line.

As I stood in line, I thought to myself, "Well, you've done it now . . . you signed yourself up. What are you going to say to these people?"

I had no idea what I was going to say. I stepped up closer in the line. I had my beliefs, but I had planned nothing. I stepped up to the podium. What had I gotten myself into?

Then something came over me.

Perhaps it was my conscience taking charge, or something beyond me, some other force greater than my fear. I heard myself saying, "Just be yourself, and I'll do the rest."

I calmed my spirit for a moment. The mayor gazed at me. Her look felt condescending and patronizing. I could almost sense her thinking, "This is a black man; he is going to be on our side."

Her face, with that demeaning, belittling expression—a look I knew well from years of enduring it from so many—is the last thing I remember seeing before I began to speak.

I had not come prepared, true, but in a greater sense I knew exactly what I was doing. I was speaking up for everyone who just wanted to be a law-abiding citizen of the United States. Everyone who wished to enjoy their God-given rights and be left alone to do it.

I stepped to the microphone—and made the speech that changed my life.

1

THE LITTLE RED HOUSE

IT STARTED out as a normal day in college. I went to class expecting the usual routine. But that day, the professor said we would do something out of the ordinary. We were going to play a game. I knew what was about to happen. I had heard people talk about this classroom exercise. We proceeded to move the tables and chairs out of the way. Then the professor asked us to stand against the wall on one side of the room.

She explained, "I will ask you a series of questions. For each question you answer with a 'yes,' you will take a certain number of steps forward. I'll tell you how many. Does everyone understand?"

I stood firm against the wall and looked around at the students. Everyone else nodded and the game began. The professor asked her first question: "Did you grow up in a household with two parents? If so, take one step forward."

Some students moved forward one step. Some students did not. I continued to stand against the wall. She asked the next question: "Did you attend a private school? If so, please take three steps forward."

Some of my classmates took those three steps forward while some stayed in place. The game continued with questions about situations we might or might not have had the opportunity to experience as children. Finally, the game ended as she asked those ahead of everyone else to turn and look at those behind. They did so.

"This," she said, "is what privilege looks like. Your privilege. Oftentimes, this is what white privilege looks like."

How many steps forward did I take? Not one. I was still leaning on that wall. The professor looked at me and laughed. "You didn't move at all. You didn't do any of these things?" she asked.

I responded, "It's not that I didn't do any of this stuff. I am just not going to play this game."

"Why not?" the professor asked. My response seemed to have surprised her. She may never have had anyone refuse to play along with the game. But I was not the typical college student. I was a grown man in my forties, as old as or even older than some of my professors. Most of the students in my class seemed to be mere kids to me.

"I am going to be honest with you," I began. "This is the stupidest thing I've seen in a long time. How can you say those people across the room are privileged just because they did all those things? Let me tell you about my childhood. I grew up in a little ramshackle, rat-infested house with a father who beat my mother, and we were dirt poor. But living in that house and in poverty, I learned more than I ever could have in a private school or on a private jet going to Europe."

I could tell that she, along with the rest of the class, didn't know what to make of my conclusion about her game. But that didn't stop me. I continued, "Let me tell you something. Those folks across the room are nowhere near as smart as I am. You know how I know? Because they were foolish enough to play this game. I was not. If they had lived like I have lived, they would have known the same thing that I know. It is not about where you come from; it is about where you end up. And being aware of that simple fact is the reason I stood against this wall and refused to be involved in this farce. Because that is exactly what this is. It is a farce."

I consider this a rule to live by. Where you come from is important, but it does not hold dominion over you. Human beings are endowed with free will and a God-given conscience. You determine where you end up.

* * *

My name is Mark Keith Robinson. I was born August 18, 1968, to Eva Mae Robinson and Dayson Johnelle Robinson at L. Richardson Memorial Hospital in Greensboro, North Carolina. I am one of ten children born to my mother, who was married twice. She had five children with her first husband. After they divorced, she married my father, a man much, much older than she was. She then had five children with him. I was the fourth of those five.

Early in my life, my three older siblings—Michael, Alice, Tony— and I were removed from our home and placed into foster care. My younger sister Gracia had not yet been born. I do not have any memories of this time, but my sister Alice tells me that Tony and I ended up in a good situation with a loving Christian woman. Michael and Alice were not so fortunate. They were placed in a home with a woman who was not very kind to them, and the woman's son was particularly mean to Michael. Alice lived in a virtual horror show. I've heard from my siblings some of the details of why we were removed from home, but I'm still not quite sure of the reasons. Yet looking back, I am sure there were several contributing factors, some of which I'll detail in a moment. Thankfully, we did not spend a huge amount of time in the foster system, and we were reunited.

That is where my real memory—and my life—begins.

I love Greensboro, North Carolina. My love for the place is part nostalgia, and part because Greensboro is a great city to live in today. It is medium-sized. I like to visit big cities, but I don't want to live in a gigantic metropolis. Greensboro is just the right size. It's a perfect mix between big city and small town. It's a town built upon the rolling hills of the North Carolina Piedmont. There are vistas and valleys. It's a town built on railroads and textile mills. The railroad tracks still divide and define it. The people are friendly. It's got enough to keep your attention, but not enough to overwhelm you. Plus, it's where my heart is.

I drive through Greensboro, and each and every part of town sparks memories. That's why I stay. Sometimes I get up on a Saturday morning or a day that I'm off, and I'll either go chase trains—I'll explain about that later—or I'll drive through my old neighborhood, the place where I grew up. Just the other day, my wife was test-driving a car. After she tried it out, I took the wheel and drove along without much of a plan. Wouldn't you know it, within minutes we ended up at 409 Dudley Street, where I spent my teenage years, across from the University of North Carolina Agriculture and Technical University—NC A&T. My hands and heart just seem to have guided me there, as they always do. But we had to get back to the lot, so I turned around. I could have kept going down Dudley Street. East on Gorrell. Past St. Stephen Church. Past Law.

To Logan Street.

To the little red house with the dirt yard.

To a place that now exists only in my mind, and in the recollections of my siblings.

Now there is just a bare lot. The house is long gone.

But back then the little red house on Logan Street was all the world to me.

This was a black section of town. We were quite poor. That's obvious to me, looking back. Yet at the time, my neighborhood was a place of mystery and wonder. Somehow, I always imagine it in the fall with leaves whipping around, the chimney fires burning, the smell of woodsmoke in the air. I picture my brothers and me walking from Windsor Community Center, or the St. Mary's School playground, with the sunset throwing long shadows before us as we head home.

Today the area is residential. This wasn't always the case. Along with an abundance of small houses, there were shops and places of business in the neighborhood in the 1970s. There were two stores we could walk to. One was called Goodson's. We went there frequently. The other was across a bridge that went over Highway 29. I didn't even remember its name. We called it "the store across the bridge." That was our boundary. Our parents told us never to go past that store. On the other side was a housing project. It formed part of a very bad neighborhood, worse than ours. And directly on the other side of that bridge was a place called the Paradise. From the way the adults talked about it, we children figured there was probably a killing down there every weekend. Bad people hung out at the Paradise. Drug dealers. Pimps and hoods. The legendary Greensboro gambler and drug dealer Slim Goody? He probably was a frequent flyer at the Paradise.

The Paradise loomed across the bridge as a foreboding marker of the bad side of town.

Logan Street was the good side, the familiar side. The neighborhood was filled with characters my siblings and I knew well and constantly discussed. The Glovers lived catty-corner to us. Lamar Glover, who was my friend, had two brothers, Rodney and Roland, who were identical twins. They would walk down the street side by side in lockstep, as if in sync. They constantly finished each other's sentences. They and Lamar all lived with their grandmother.

Around the corner were the Swans. Nearby lived a man who looked like a black version of the wrestler Dusty Rhodes—which caused my brothers and me to admire him greatly. Beyond him on the street lived an older woman who sat on her porch in a long, old-fashioned dress, looking like Celie from *The Color Purple*. As I later learned, she ran the "liquor house" in the neighborhood. At the corner lived a fellow we called Precious Man, because he was always complaining about everyone and everything around him. What made him so special, we wondered.

Lamar and I used to climb a big tree in front of my house and sit in the branches, sometimes for hours. The main reason we did this was to talk and joke, but the tree also provided a vantage point. There was a girl in the neighborhood we had a crush on. Her name was Belle Johnson.

Oh, Belle Johnson! Belle Johnson was a high school student and much older than we were. At that point in my life, she was the prettiest girl I'd ever seen. We used to sit in the tree and wait for her to come outside. She drove a Mopar-orange Monte Carlo with a black top. She used to drive that car with her knee while eating an orange of a slightly lighter color than her car. Lamar and I argued about which one of us was going to marry Belle when we grew up. Alas, she moved away and ended up marrying a professional basketball player by the name of Gene Banks who later became a legendary coach.

There were more terrifying neighborhood characters, such as Riser Boy, who was a really threatening-looking dude we saw sometimes, and the more mythological Eat the Bread, who was a child molester who would grab you if you went in the wrong place. There was a drunkard we called Pee Wee because he would stagger around the neighborhood and say, "Pee Wee. Pee Wee," over and over. I heard about him long before I encountered him—but encounter him I did. I had a bike back then, but my bike didn't have a chain guard. Once I was riding it and my pants got caught in the chain. Down I went. I was lying on the ground trying to yank my pants out of my chain when I heard, "Peeee Weeeee." It was like a horror movie. I yanked at my snarled pants, struggled like crazy to work them free, all the while thinking, "Pee Wee's gonna get me!" I pictured him as an eyeless creature with no teeth.

As I was screaming at the top my lungs, my brother Michael ran up to help. While he was pulling me free, Pee Wee slunk behind us and I watched him walk away.

Just a man. Some poor old drunk. At the time, however, I was sure I'd barely escaped death.

Logan Street is narrow. It barely allows two cars to pass. As I mentioned, the house no longer exists, but the lot is still there. It seems tiny now. The house couldn't have been much larger than an average suburban living room these days. We had a small garden. My father sometimes grew watermelons in the back. We had no grass except on the edge of the curb by the street. Other than that, the front and back yards were black dirt, which we kept raked. In the very back was the Junk House, where my father kept his tools. It was tiny, at the most five-foot-by-nine, but it seemed huge to us. It was very junky, very dark. We ventured in to frighten ourselves sometimes, but this was the domain of my father.

There was always the smell of cooking—and not just any cooking. What I remember most is the aroma of pinto beans. Even today, the smell of pinto beans simmering on a stove can instantly take me back to those times. That's the way I remember Logan Street most fondly. I always seem to imagine it in autumn. I remember the smell of a big old pot of pinto beans cooking on a fall afternoon. Outside the day is overcast and chilly, and I would get a whiff of those pinto beans as I walked past the kitchen, out of the warm house, and into the chilly outside air. Once outside I was surrounded by the smell of chimney smoke and the pungent odor of freshly fallen leaves. And I'd take a few steps and hear the crackle of those dried leaves underfoot. Those are the days that I remember.

For me, cereal was pivotal, a big memory from my childhood. The crackle of Frosted Flakes and Captain Crunch can still take me back. And oh, we put sugar on our cereal then, whether it was sweetened or not! My cereals of choice growing up were Frosted Flakes, Captain Crunch, and Quisp, with the alien on the box.

Hot chocolate with buttery toast. Pork chops.

"Biscuits and syrup," Alice reminds me.

"Yes, and not that Mrs. Butterworth's garbage," I might add. "Karo. Pure corn syrup!"

Apple pie.

My mother once baked an apple pie. When it was done she pulled it out of the oven, and my father asked her to slice him a piece. She set it in front of him and my dad took a bite of that lava-hot apple pie. A look of agony came over his face. He spat it out, then angrily slapped the pie across the room. "Damn your apple pie!" he shouted.

Of course he was quite willing to eat my mother's apple pie once it had cooled.

Sound idyllic? Not always.

While my mother had ten children in total, I grew up accustomed to having five or six of us in the house at one time. Michael, Alice, and Tony were there, and my younger sister Gracia. My sister Debbie was transitional in our lives. While we loved her none the less, she seemed to fade in and out of the home. Eventually she left the Greensboro area, got married, and now lives in Indiana.

My mother and father were both present in the home until my father died. But having a two-parent home did not lead to a balanced, well-adjusted life. My father was an alcoholic, and when he drank he became violent towards my mother. The weekends would roll around, and my father would go to the liquor store and purchase enough for the next few days. He would spend the weekends drunk and abusive. I witnessed unfair fights as my father, who was a very large man, beat my mother. I remember thinking to myself as a child that it simply was not fair that a man as big and muscular as my dad should hit my much smaller mother.

He was strong. I once watched my father pick up a lawnmower with one hand and throw it across the yard. No man should beat a woman, but especially not a man who is that large and strong. My mother was always instructing us to play fair with one another. Yet I watched this unfair fight in which she was forced to engage. Even as a child, I felt the imbalance, the wrongness of it. At an early age, I began to think of the world in terms of what is fair or unfair, right or wrong.

Yet while I believe that there is a definite right or wrong, sometimes what's needed is to examine a particular situation with understanding and love to arrive at a correct judgement. Intelligence must be applied to questions of justice. My parents are a good example. They were complex people, and their relationship was far from stereotypical. For one thing, my father was at least twenty-four years older than my mother. Dayson Johnelle was born in Charleston, South Carolina, in 1904 (we think), but he lived a lot of his life in Florida before eventually settling down with my mother in North Carolina. We aren't sure of his history in Florida. My father never talked about it, at least not to us. We know he was in prison at some point, because my mom used to tell us stories about him being "on the chain gang." My father wore a hearing aid, and my brother Tony says that his hearing was damaged when a sheriff hit him in the side of the head while arresting him. Alice, on the other hand, remembers being told his deafness was caused by gunfire next to his ear.

My cousin George told me that he left Florida because he killed two deputy sheriffs. This would have been after his time in jail, I suppose. He may have had a Native American mother—a Blackfoot Indian, so the story goes—and a half-black, half-Irish father.

None of this is substantiated. I know very little.

According to what we think is his armed forces draft registration card during World War II, he was an employee at a tourist camp in Winter Haven, Florida. The card puts him at forty-four years of age, but his death certificate claims he was born in 1904. It could be he was back-dating the card so he would be past draft age. Nevertheless, by the time I was born in 1968, Dad was either sixty-four or perhaps even several years older than that. Contrast that with my mother, who was forty.

But man, was he ever robust for his age. That lawnmower I saw him throw across the yard? He did that while in his seventies. My father was primarily a carpenter by trade but was generally a whiz at dealing with anything mechanical. He was fast with arithmetic as well. He could look at a column of numbers and quickly add it in his head. That is not a trait I inherited.

Dad could fix anything. He had a side business repairing lawn mowers and appliances. A neighbor of ours, a hardheaded World War II veteran, had brought that lawnmower in for repair. He was a skinny man who walked with a limp. I knew he was a former soldier because I remember him snapping a salute at me and chiding me for not knowing how to return it. Believe me, in the coming years I would learn very well how to return a salute!

My father took one look at the ancient mower and told him it was too old and he should get a new one, but the other fellow was determined: that mower could be fixed. It *would* be fixed. For some reason, my father agreed to take it on, despite his misgivings. He tried for weeks to get the thing working, but as he'd known from the start, it was beyond repair.

Still, he hemmed and hawed about returning it until the old vet came storming into the yard one day demanding his mower back and punctuated this by calling my dad a string of terrible curse words.

I was sitting near a stump in our dirtpack backyard, playing with little green army men and watching as my dad turned with a ballpeen hammer in his hand. Dad told the man to take the mower away with him. The man wouldn't give up.

"You told me you would fix that mower, and there it is still sitting there. You're just a—" and the cursing continued.

With a returning string of profanity that might have set my young ears burning had I not heard all the words before, Dad picked up the mower from the bench where he had it—this was a good-sized power mower, but without the push handle attached. He grabbed it by the cowl over the pull cable and flung it across our dirt-paved yard, nearly making it to the fence. The old vet was stunned. He went away with his mower. He was grumbling but did not challenge my father any further. Even in his seventies, Dad was a formidable presence.

My mother, at about five foot, six inches, was not on a physical par with my father but was no shrinking violet herself. For me as a child, she was perfect and perfectly in the right. She would and did fight back when accosted by my father—although it was never a fair fight, as he was simply larger and stronger than she was. Usually, however, their fights were merely verbal. It was when my father drank that he became dangerous.

The truth is, though I have characterized him as an alcoholic at times, I am not entirely sure he was addicted in that way. He drank on weekends and holidays. He didn't go to work drunk, and he wasn't drunk during the week. But when he drank, he drank heavily, and the effect was not a good one.

My siblings and I have speculated that it was Dad's native intelligence and ambitious nature that made him such a bad drunk. He was a very smart man. He was intelligent at a time when black men were not *supposed* to be intelligent. This no doubt left him continually frustrated. My siblings and I feel that, had he been born into different times, he might have achieved a great deal more. For instance, I often think that if he had been born when I was born, it might be my dad sitting in the North Carolina lieutenant governor's position instead of me. Maybe he knew this about himself.

He once made Tony and me pairs of wings out of some cardboard. They were for attaching to our backs. Like most things he did, they were well-crafted. He had us go up on the roof of the house and jump off to test them and see if we could glide down. At the time I was more worried about breaking a leg than figuring out if the wings worked, but it's an example of the imagination and drive of the man, as well as his desire to share this with us, his children. There seemed to be something inside my dad that was supposed to come out that never did. All his frustration *did* come out when he drank, however, and violence was sometimes the result.

It was that violence that led to Alice, Michael, Tony, and me landing in foster care for those five months, February to June of 1970.

I was too young to remember, but according to my sister Alice and my brother Michael, the feuding between my parents culminated in the worst fight they ever had. My father's anger and frustration, never far beneath the surface, got the better of him, and he attacked my mother, hitting her in the head with the butt of a gun, and threatened more violence. She called the police on him and fled to her mother's to protect herself. My father was not generally a danger to us children, at least not in the physical sense (although my brother Michael still bears the scar from the time my father popped him on the head with a can as a punishment for crying too much when a toddler). For the most part, Dad's wrath was directed at my mother. After my mother left, the police responded to the incident, and my father was taken to jail for a time. We four were put in foster care (my youngest sister Gracia had not yet been born). Thankfully, we did not spend a large amount of time in the foster system—only a few months—and we were reunited on Logan Street in Greensboro. My mother and father reconciled, as they always did throughout the tumultuous years of their marriage, and we all returned.

Again, I know very little about my dad and mother's relationship.

By the time I was old enough to notice such things and try to puzzle them out, my father had died. I don't even know how the two met. And neither do any of my siblings. Nevertheless, despite the eruptions of violence, they stayed together, and Gracia was born in 1972.

As I mentioned, my sister Alice and brothers Michael and Tony remember foster care very well. My half-sister Debbie was placed along with Alice. All of them hated it. Alice and Michael had absolutely terrible experiences, and my sister had an experience that was quite abusive. Among other instances, her foster mother's sixteen-year-old granddaughter tied nine-year-old Alice down to a bench naked with belts and hit and violated her with a shoe. Meanwhile, the foster mother would constantly threaten to throw Alice "into the rosebush" if she acted up.

A few years later, Alice's foster parents came by the house for some reason, and, according to my sister, my father, who had heard about his daughter and stepdaughter's treatment from Debbie, confronted them with a shotgun and ordered them to leave.

"He's gonna shoot 'em, gonna shoot 'em!" Alice remembers Debbie shouting with glee.

Ten-year-old Michael too had to endure a smug bully in the form of the son of his foster mother. Years later, when he was in his thirties, Michael learned that the young man had soon after drowned in a pond and, although other foster kids were present, no one tried to save him.

I was placed in the same house with my brother Tony, who was five at the time. We were in a decent place, although Tony did grow homesick and tried to run away to home one day. He only got to the edge of the neighborhood before his foster mother located him. Of course, at the time there was no home to return to. If we had not eventually been reunited, it is hard to say what kind of life I might have had. So much of my own character has its foundation in my relationship with my four full siblings and our life together. Despite our age differences, for many years we were quite an inseparable unit.

The fight between my father and mother that resulted in our family separation may have been the worst, but it was certainly not the last, and I *do* remember those. Some may believe that witnessing domestic violence in my home would result in one of two outcomes: either I would be abusive as an adult, or I would be fiercely against the use of physical force in any form. However, neither is true. By most definitions, violence has negative connotations. And in most situations, yes, violence is bad. But is violent behavior ever necessary?

At home, I saw when my mom eventually used physical force against my dad. After years of abuse, she knew she had to fight back to protect herself. She responded violently to my father's abuse, but only as a reaction, to strike back in a very unfair struggle. To defend herself, she found that a form of violent behavior was at times necessary. Her motive was not to injure my father, yet I know he occasionally received physical pain from her retaliation.

Am I implying that violence is the answer to violence? No. But is violence sometimes necessary? Yes. So what's the difference? The difference is having the wisdom to know when violence is necessary and for what reasons. My mother knew when to use violent physical force. Her motives were not malicious; she was driven by self-preservation. Through my young eyes, I began to see violence as something that just happens, many times unnecessarily, but at other times unavoidably.

My father may have been complicated and frustrated. He may have been disappointed in life. My mother may have reminded him of his own failings; she may even have taunted him with them on occasion. But he should never have used his greater physical strength to harm my mother. I believe that men have this particular responsibility from God, since he gave us greater physical stature. My mother was completely justified in defending herself.

Many today say that violence is never necessary. I disagree. Watching my father beat my mother and seeing my mom fight back for her life taught me that wisdom is always necessary when deciding the moral rightness of using physical force. I pray the day will never come, though I realize it may, when I must exercise that wisdom to protect myself or my own.

Some may ask, did I ever step in to stop my father? The answer is no. Why not? Well, various reasons. Even though I knew it was not fair for my dad to beat my mom, it was the norm in our home. Furthermore, my father was the authority figure in our home. And the truth is, for the most part my mother wanted him to be. Even as a child, I knew there would always be someone to answer to, and in my house that person was my dad. He was the final authority. There were times when my mother struggled to get us to obey; but it only took a stern glance from dad to rein us in. So no, I never intervened. I dared not challenge his authority. I'm a large man these days. Some have even called me imposing (among other things). Keep in mind that my father died when I was twelve. Back then, of course, I was just a little boy. I simply stayed out of the way.

The little red house on Logan Street was a rental. It had four rooms total. There was a living room, a kitchen, and two bedrooms. My parents had one bedroom, and the four of us, later the five of us, had the other bedroom. On the back porch was a washing machine, and we hung clothes on the line to dry. In our bedroom, there was a bunkbed. Alice slept on the top bunk, and Tony on the bottom. Michael had his own bed, and I had a small bed next to Tony's. We also had a long monstrosity of a dresser we all shared.

Michael reminds me that our father's favorite food was boiled chicken. Michael always sat beside Dad at the table, and this made Michael nervous—yet my mother determined the seating arrangements at our table, and that is where my mother put him. Michael would eat quickly, and this sometimes upset his stomach. He had a habit of throwing up. But by the time I was old enough to remember anything, my father was past such tantrums toward us children.

The one time I was afraid my dad was going to kill me was when I hit my brother Tony in the head with a rock. We got into a fight, and I was mad, so I threw a rock. It was one of the big crumbly rocks that were down at Windsor Center, a park with an activity structure where we played. I didn't mean to hit him in the head, but I did. Right in the side of the head. Tony still has a scar on the right side from it. It was a big gash. I threw it so hard it could've killed him. Alice was there and walked home with him bleeding, and I walked behind, crying a lot more than Tony was. I was also shaking and thinking, "I'm going to die when I get home." When I got home my father indeed tried to give me what would have been the epic whooping of all time, no doubt, but my mom saved me. That's the only time he ever came after me.

That is also one of the few fights Tony and I got into. Normally when we were mad, we did something we called "passing licks," which was repeatedly whacking each other on the shoulder back and forth. We'd keep that up until Mama stopped us and maybe gave us a small whipping. We very seldom actually hurt one another. "We were a tribe unto ourselves," my brother Tony says. "We created our own rules and lived our own way. Everybody else out there could go crazy, experimenting with drugs and everything, and we were sitting in the house reenacting scenes from our favorite movies."

And spinning around to get high. That's how we got high, by going into the front yard, looking up, and spinning around. Then while lying down on the ground. "I'm wasted," we'd proclaim. Then after a while, "Oh, I'm okay. Let's do it again." I highly recommend it. A cheap high with no side effects!

"It's interesting to think about how narrow that street was, and how close the houses were. They were very small," Tony says. "It was almost like an apartment building. Everybody knew everybody. I'll never forget the night Mrs. Johnson had a heart attack. The EMS was there, and they were working on her. It seemed like it was happening in our house. Then they wheeled her out and took her away, and later that night we got word that she had died. It was like a member of our family had died. That's what it felt like, an extended family."

There was also a lot to see. All you had to do was look up. I've always been fascinated by trains and airplanes. I used to constantly check for airplanes flying over. Man, I used to love seeing one. Once when Gracie was sitting in the front yard, she was looking up and saying, "Hey, airplane, hey airplane." So I jumped off the porch and went out to see what she was talking about. I looked up . . . and it was the Goodyear blimp. You would have thought somebody had sold me all of California, I was so happy. I ran across the street following it, and before I knew it, I was far up the street past St. Stephen Church. That was where I turned around and came back, repeating over and over to myself, "Man, I saw the Goodyear blimp!"

The first time I flew in a plane was when I was eighteen, leaving Charlotte to go to Texas to enter the Army and attend basic training. I flew on Piedmont Airlines—which is out of business and has been absorbed into another airline now. We went to Dallas–Fort Worth on a short, fat 727, then to Fort Bliss, which is in El Paso—a city I will long contend is the weirdest place on Earth. I used to walk out of my barracks—Third Platoon barracks in the quadrangle at Logan Heights—stand on the porch, and look straight ahead. I could see dusty, crowded Juarez, Mexico. Then I looked left, and I could see the Chihuahuan Desert stretching into New Mexico. And when I looked right, there were mountains. Always at the top of those mountains there was either rain or snow. I would ask myself, "How in the world is it 100 degrees down here, and there's snow at the top of those things?"

It was a long way from Greensboro.

* * *

The little red house had air conditioning. It was called rain. The rain would cool the place down very nicely for a few minutes, then it was back to Greensboro heat. There was a big industrial fan in one of the windows of the house. It lacked a grill, and I'm amazed none of us fell into the blades while roughhousing and got chopped up. The fan had a metal housing that my father had painted green. There was a smaller box fan we sat on the floor. I hate to say it, but we would occasionally chase a mouse into it. The thing was, there were quite a few mice and rats infesting the house at times. This was a hazard of the entire neighborhood. I particularly remember a night—we called it *Ben Hur* night because that's what we were watching on our black-and-white television—when we chased several mice into the box fan. This did not go well for the mice, and we disposed of them outside. Meanwhile in the kitchen, a rat trap popped over and over again, killing larger rodents. Of course at the time this all seemed perfectly natural to us. Now my brothers and sisters laugh at those days. *Now* we realize the conditions in which we lived. It is no exaggeration. We *were* poor. Very poor. But we had each other to depend on, and that is how we made it through.

We had no phone for many years. We finally had central air when we moved to 411 Dudley Street, a house next door to our original 409 Dudley Street rental, in 1983. We did get a phone not long before my father died. We had cars only intermittently; then they broke or we had to sell them, and we did not have a car for long stretches of time.

We did have one mode of transportation other than walking. Throughout my childhood all of us children had bicycles, supplied by my father, who built them himself from spare parts. Alice rode a bike with a big basket on front that was actually my father's, but she often used it to bring back things from the store in the basket. We went around as a group on our bicycles too.

Not all my memories of bicycling are happy ones. I once had a tragic accident on the bicycle my father made for me when I rode it downtown. I remember the day well: riding downtown, riding among all those downtown folks. They seemed very important, going about their business with important Greensboro downtown things to do. And as I was watching them, I went off the curb and—*bam!*

My bicycle broke in half. It just came apart at a seam and fell into two parts, leaving me lying in the street, looking up at the sky. I wasn't badly hurt, but I was terribly embarrassed. I remember carrying the bike home and mumbling to myself, "Not only did I look like a fool in front of all those downtown folks, now I have to go home and get a beating."

Well, that didn't happen, and Dad eventually fixed the bicycle for me. I didn't take it downtown for a very long time afterward, however.

Despite the poverty and the occasional violence, I would not trade my childhood on Logan Street for anything. It isn't so much what happens to you when you are young as it is what you make of it. I would not say that I have had a good life despite my childhood. I would say it's been good *because* of the lessons and memories I chose to take with me from that impressionable time. That is part of what I was trying to communicate to my professor when she asked me why I didn't take part in her "privilege walk" along with the rest of the class. I consider my poor childhood, a childhood sometimes disrupted by violence, not as a legacy that drags me down but as an advantage I can draw upon to lift myself and others up.

2

LOGAN STREET DAYS

MY PARENTS fought over all manner of things. They fought over the names of their children. For many years, my sister Gracia was "Baby" or "the baby." Even though my birth certificate bears the name I have, my parents couldn't decide on what to call me for some time. My dad told my mother when she went to the hospital with me to name me *Hercules*. That would not be good after *The Nutty Professor* came out. When I tell people that, some of them will start up the chant from that movie, "Hercules, Hercules!" I would definitely have to go to the gym often if that were my name.

When my mother came home with me, and told him she had not named me Hercules, he was furious. Where did he come up with that name? It was one of many seemingly odd things my father knew and did. Someone once asked me in an interview if I could sit down and talk to anybody, who would it be? I told them I would like to sit down and talk to my dad and speak to him when he was at his sharpest mentally. I'd be willing to bet he comprehended stuff that people would be shocked that he knew.

The matter of my name was finally settled when Mrs. Shelton, the guidance counselor from Washington Street Elementary, registered me as Mark Keith Robinson. Another presence in our life at the time was Richard Fogelman, the local truant officer. At the time, the school system was transitioning truant officers into social workers, so his job title changed. But he had identified us as "at-risk students"—aka po' kids—and if we didn't show up for school, he might drop by and we had to tell him, "Mr. Fogelman, I was sitting eating crackers and soup and watching *Price Is Right* and I had the flu." Before I was born, or at least before I remember anything, Mrs. Shelton and Mr. Fogelman paid particular attention to my brother Michael and sister Alice, treating them almost like relatives. Mrs. Shelton took Alice and Michael to the zoo once, for example. We thought they were rich. They had cars, after all.

My father's love for my mom was a very jealous one. For example, he would not allow my mom to go to church. My mom wanted to go and wanted her children to attend as well. Dad did not mind the kids going to church and would allow my mom's friend, Grace, to pick us up and take us. But he would not let my mom attend. He had no interest in going to church himself and was afraid my mom would meet another man there. His answer was to keep her home. Looking back, I understand how that twenty-four-year (or possibly greater) difference between him and my mother might have been preying on his mind. He'd married her while still feeling in his prime, I'm sure, but age caught up with him. My mother would live on for many decades. He himself wasn't long for the world. When I think back on the relationship between my mom and my dad, it's no longer a melodramatic "good guy, bad guy" thing. It was much more than "My dad got drunk and beat up on my mom." This does not excuse the violence. There is no excuse for that. But when you look past it, you see there was a lot more going on than somebody getting drunk and beating someone else up.

The complicated relationship my mother had with my sisters illustrates this. My mother treated us boys differently than the girls. We were princes. Honestly, I could for the most part do no wrong in my mother's eyes. I probably could have gone out and shot somebody dead, and my mama still wouldn't have judged me. She probably would have said, "Well, that's all right baby, that guy called you a bad name. I'll be with you every day at the trial, and I'll come see you and bring you cigarettes in prison."

My sister Alice and my mother were often at odds, however. She was critical of the girls and had low expectations for them. At the same time, she expected much more personal attention from them than from the boys. As Alice reminds me, she herself was very close to my father. They would often play checkers at the kitchen table. She would often spend time watching him fix things in the back. Alice feels that my mother was often expecting, almost hoping, that Alice would mess up, get in trouble, perhaps get pregnant or get into drugs, so my mother could then say, "I told you so." My relationship with Mom was the opposite. I felt completely supported.

Before he died, my father tried to explain to my mom why he beat her. He said that he loved her so much, and that was the only way he knew to express it. Never in a million years will I understand that way of thinking, but perhaps he learned that type of love during his childhood. By God's grace, I am thankful I took another path altogether.

My father's love for his children was expressed through gifts. We didn't have much money, but my dad would buy small items to give to me, and I recognized this as his way of saying he loved me. My dad had been a carpenter, a construction worker, and a builder. He was retired, receiving social security and a meager pension by the time I was born. He would still do odd jobs to supplement his income. This was why he began to repair lawn mowers. We received government subsidized food staples to help feed the hungry mouths. I remember my older brothers and sisters going to the railroad station to pick up the food the government would provide.

As my brother Michael reminds me, it wasn't the railroad station itself where we obtained the food, but a storage warehouse behind it. The place was on Plott Street near Washington Street. The food came in black-and-white boxes with black lettering on them: powdered milk, peanut butter, cheese, nonperishable items. The last time they ever did this was a food pickup down at the stadium when they were giving out big boxes of "government cheese," paid for, I later learned, by the American taxpayer in the form of subsidies to the dairy industry that led to overproduction. But that government cheese was good stuff.

I also have memories of going to the grocery store to buy food with money from my dad's social security check. Just as now, social security checks came once a month. Looking back, it seems we lived a higher life for the first week after his check came, and then struggled the more the month went on. For a long time in the late 1970s there was very, very little money to feed a household of seven, which included five growing children.

The lack of material goods brought my brothers and sisters and me closer together because we didn't have money to do a lot of things. As my brother Tony says, "We were a tribe unto ourselves." What we had was a living room and television set we all gathered around. Each of us had his or her spot. Alice, who of all the kids was probably the closest to my dad, sat near him. The rest of us were spaced out around the screen. It may have been the 1970s, but our television was black and white. We only had an antenna, no cable. We might have to adjust the antenna's direction depending on what channel we were watching. There were three channels we could regularly get, and three others we could pick up if we moved the antenna the right way.

It sounds primitive today, but you had to watch what was on. *The ABC Sunday Night Movie, The Wonderful World of Disney,* whatever. There were recurring movies that would come around every year such as *King Kong, West Side Story,* and *Night of the Grizzly.* We saw the *Ten Commandments* every Easter, and *Ben Hur* and *The Wizard of Oz.* We watched reruns in the afternoons. There are so many television shows that I look back on now and think "Why did I ever sit through that?" *Happy Days* is an example. It is unwatchable for me as an adult. On the other hand, some shows get better with age. I can watch *Gunsmoke* anytime now and enjoy it. That opening: gun shots, and then the camera pulls back. Matt Dillon has had to take out some very bad guy. Then he'll look at the camera and shake his head in disappointment as if to say, "I hated to do that."

As my brother Tony points out, that was my father's favorite show.

My father never went to the doctor. However, one day in 1979 my dad asked my mom to take him to the hospital. I knew there had to be something wrong, for this was the first time I had ever seen him seek medical attention. We now lived on Dudley Street, and the hospital, L. Richardson Memorial, was not far from the house. I felt that I could almost see it from my upstairs bedroom window, a window that faced the house's lot. I knew which direction the hospital lay because it was also the direction of our old house on Logan Street. I remember sitting in that window and looking toward the hospital, confused and sad, knowing my dad was there. Yet I could not fully process my sadness. It wasn't like I had an intimate relationship with him. We didn't have deep conversations. I didn't go to him with my problems. We simply were not that close. Yet I was concerned for my dad. It was a feeling of dread. I got a horrible sense that something bad was going to happen. I started crying uncontrollably. I couldn't stop for a long time. My mother heard me. She came in and consoled me until I finally fell asleep.

The next day, I woke to found out my father was dead.

It had taken one day. He'd gone in the afternoon before and died in the early morning hours. I'm not sure what he died from. My brother Michael says the cause of death was cirrhosis of the liver. My father was listed as dying at seventy-five. He may have been older—perhaps much older. His birth year is listed as 1904, but it could be that the date on his draft card is right, and he was six years older. We don't really know. My mother and Alice accompanied him to L. Richardson in a borrowed car. Alice remembers her last moment with him. He saw she was excited by the vending machines, and he gave her a dollar to buy something, telling her to get change from her mother.

He had a hard time through the night according to my brother

Tony. At one point the hospital called to tell my mother that they couldn't get him to accept treatment and that they were having a difficult time with him. I don't think the illness was a direct result of his vices. He had cut back on his drinking by this time in his life. In 1974 he'd quit smoking cold turkey. Maybe the decades of hard living before that had taken their toll on his older self.

When my father died, I was only twelve years old. His death horrified me. I worried about how we were going to make it now. Could we even eat without him? My mother did not work. My father had always controlled the purse strings. Were we going to have to live on the streets? How would we survive?

My mother did not remarry after my father's death. She remained a single widowed woman. At the time of his death, there were five of us children in school, ranging from third grade to high school. My mom once told me that a friend of hers, who lived down the street, came to her when my father died.

"You know," she said, "now that your husband is dead you can just live off welfare. You can just sit back and get all kinds of checks."

But my mother stepped up. I mean, she really stepped up. She did not plan to depend on welfare. She planned on going to work. But how was a woman who was not a skilled laborer and had only a fifth grade education going to earn a living?

My mother had friends who worked at NC A&T. She asked them about work at the college. They were able to direct her to a job as a custodian. She walked to work and walked home. Early in her working days, food could run low in the house. I remember one day in particular during summer break; Mom was working, and my siblings and I were at home. We were hungry, and every TV commercial for food looked like the best thing we could imagine. Then my mom received her first paycheck. That afternoon, she surprised us by going to McDonald's to use her money to buy us hamburgers, french fries, apple pies, and sundaes. She bought us everything we'd ever desired, or so it seemed! I even got a Big Mac. That was probably the best meal I've had in my whole life. Before then I couldn't remember even eating in a restaurant. That night was a turning point for our family. We realized that we would make it without my dad. At the time, it was just about a hamburger. That Big Mac was like heaven, like hitting the lottery. But now, as an adult, I recognize it was about so much more than. It was about my mother's commitment to us.

My mother was from Burgaw, North Carolina, a farming community thirty miles north of Wilmington, which is North Carolina's major port city. My brother Tony most often accompanied her back to her home area to visit relatives and attend funerals and such. He remembers her pointing out landmarks of her childhood.

"That's the field I used to walk across when my mama sent me to the store, and I used to walk across it that way."

"She was always a little bit like that child all her life," says Tony. "Her virtues and her vices were very childlike. And that's the way I still think of her. As a child. She had a child's innocence. And in a way that made it tougher to go through all the things she did in her life."

My mother came from a very different world than we did, even living poor in Greensboro in the 1970s. I'll have to explain what the term "color-struck" means. It is differentiation based on the degree of lightness or darkness of one's skin—that is, a black person's skin. Being color-struck is a social ill that still afflicts many black people to this day. This often surprises those who are unaware of it, but I assure you it is quite real. In the past it was worse. For example, when my mother was growing up in Burgaw and my grandmother needed to go to the store in town, she would not take my mother and her siblings along. Instead, she would "borrow" a neighbor's kids and take them with her. Think about that; she took a neighbor's kids. Why? My grandmother was lighter skinned. My grandfather was very dark in complexion—I remember once thinking that he looked almost like an old black shoe—and all the kids were more his skin tone. My grandmother knew she would be treated better if she came into the store with lighter skinned children. Also those kids "matched" her more. And so my mother stayed at home when my grandmother went shopping. Having experiences like that remained with her throughout her life. Yet instead of handicapping her, they gave her the will to endure. If you can make it through being shut inside as a small child by your mother because your skin isn't the right shade of brown, you can make it through a lot of other setbacks and slights in life.

To me, my mother always seemed to have a damper on her personal expectations, but she had great expectations for me. As for herself, she never seemed to want to be too happy, because then something was bound to go wrong. And so many times in her life, it did. Above all, my mother was a source of love and care for me. As a poor kid, I was often low on self-esteem, but I was seldom low on self-respect, which is a different and better quality. I owe this to my mother. I always felt loved and cared for.

There were other changes at home after my father's death. My mother's friend Grace Hinnet invited her to go to church, and now my mother felt she could do so. So not only did my mom go to work, she also began to attend church. Without my father to stop her, she became very active at Saint Stephen United Church of Christ. She sang in the choir and was a part of all the ladies' circles. Looking back, that church was a positive constant in my life as a child. I loved being in that place. I looked up to many people there.

St. Stephen was located within walking distance of our house. It is a Protestant church. The United Church of Christ was heavily involved in the civil rights movement. It continues to be a church that is very socially progressive. That's part of the reason that I took my family out of that church in later years. I believe some things ought to be changed, but some matters are always going to be a sin. When we attended, the church was very traditional. We didn't have a gospel choir. We didn't have drums, tambourines, or any of the stuff you see in a so-called "black church." We had a pipe organ. We sang standard hymns: "Holy, Holy, Holy," and "Amazing Grace." Those are songs I still love. While people were very expressive, with words like "amen" and "hallelujah" often ringing out, it wasn't this—dare I say—caricature of jumping in the aisles and running around. Some people might even call it a "white church." The only problem with that characterization is that everyone who attended was black!

When I was younger, there was a lot of Biblical teaching. But I feel the direction of the church started going sideways when the pastor I grew up with, Dr. George Gay, retired. He was very conservative, very straight in the Word. He was an influence on me. He was not charismatic in the emotional sense; he was no-nonsense and could even be seen as grouchy. His sermons were always based strictly not on his opinion alone, but on the Bible and biblical truth.

In our church, everything was done right and in order, something I still strongly believe in. As my brother Michael remembers, some Caucasian people once visited during the week and asked Dr. Gay, "Is this a white church in a black community?" Dr. Gay's answer was, "No, this is a church in a community." Someone once asked me something similar. "Do you go to a white church or a black church."

"It's brick," was my reply.

It was important for me that so many members were black, however. It was my first glimpse of normal black life, a place where people weren't extremely poor and everything difficult. That was the first place I saw black people who had money or wore military uniforms. When I was still of middle school age, I saw a man in navy dress blues in the narthex of the church. I was fascinated. I followed him all around the church.

There were men in that church who took me under their wings, so to speak. There was one man, Eddie Hargrove, who became a father figure to me. He had worked at A&T as a professor but was retired by the time I came along. The conversations I never had with my dad, I was able to have with him. He mentored me. He knew I had done public speaking at school (more on that in a moment). He used to pay me to do work around his house during the summer. I think the reason he did was twofold. More than anything, he was concerned about trying to give me direction. Second, he was trying to keep me from getting into any kind of trouble. During those times he would talk to me about life,

27

struggles, and whatever was on my mind. He was the first person who told me that when you walk into a room and see people wearing suits and ties, don't think those people are smarter than you. "Some of the dumbest people you ever meet will have on a necktie and polished shoes."

I also distinctly remember him telling me, "Don't have children until you get married and have some money in your pocket. Once you have children, you have to go to work. One of the worst sins, unforgiveable, is not to take care of your children."

He was medium brown, tall man. For his age, he was in very good shape. He knew so much about the world. He knew about brick masonry. He owned his house free and clear. The neighborhood he lived in on Ross Avenue in the Benbow Road area was filled with black professionals: teachers, doctors, and lawyers. His house was certainly the nicest house I'd ever seen owned by a black person.

Eddie Hargrove and others were mentors to me. They, along with my older siblings, helped me to understand that the evil and injustice in this world were the result of man's disobedience. That, along with my mother's constant assertion that our faith in God would get us through, helped me to grow and never blame God for life's shortcomings.

Church also provided me the opportunity to see successful people, people who didn't seem to be struggling every step of the way. There was one man there named Karl. He was tall and strong. He had been in the military, a Marine in Vietnam, and then worked for the post office. I would look at Karl and think, "Man, I want to be just like him when I grow up." But as a child, I had no idea how I could ever be like Karl. Nonetheless, I looked up to him and many others there. Those were the kind of people we went to church with at St. Stephen. They were people of means. They had money and jobs and careers and families. They served as an inspiration to me. I always wanted to be like the people at church.

This was so important to me. I make a joke sometimes: "Choosy people choose Jif. And so do we." That's the way I felt back then. "People" meant *other* people. People downtown. People on television. I wasn't "people."

But as I got older, I started coming out of that, and the people at St. Stephen were a pivotal part of providing direction and inspiration for my life.

Black lives mattered then. They mattered to one young man who was desperately looking for an exemplar, a model for how to live and behave. Nobody at St. Stephen was trying to act black or white. Nobody was forced into any role they didn't choose by some nebulous societal force. They were being themselves of their own free wills and living happy and successful lives. That's what I wanted for myself.

Saint Stephen UCC provided a safe haven when things in my life were uncertain. That church and my mom's constant supervision of who her children spent time around were major influencing factors in my worldview.

Would it have been easier for my mom to sit at home, wait for government checks to show up in the mail, seclude herself from society, and not strive to build a strong foundation for her children? Sure, probably so. But if she had done that, nothing would have gotten *better*. And it did get better. My mom walked to work each day to clean toilets and mop floors so that her children would have a home, food, and clothing. My mom diligently supervised us and instructed us in right and wrong. She consistently afforded us opportunities to be influenced by faithful Christians to help us grow and mature.

I knew, even then, that my mom was doing all of that for us. But now, as an adult, I fully understand what my mother went through. She sacrificed. And more than that, she inspired her children. She taught us life lessons by her example that could only have come amidst the trials we experienced. I was never ashamed of my mother. She was a widowed single woman who had a fifth-grade education, five children in the home, ten children total, and very meager resources. Yet she managed to provide a good life for her family. We never had much, but we always had satisfied stomachs, electricity, and water. Beyond that we had a few extras. We never went without Christmas gifts, and eventually Mom would end up purchasing two different homes and multiple vehicles in her lifetime. This did not always go well. She got in over her head with her first mortgage and lost the house (it was another house on Dudley Street). This might have been the end of the dream of ownership for some people. But for my mother, it was another setback to overcome. She eventually purchased another house, and, having a better idea of how mortgages and financing work, kept that one.

We even got air conditioning!

I saw my mother work miracles with the scraps handed to her and the giants before her. This planted deep within me an appreciation for working hard and not living a life reliant on government assistance. I have had my own personal ups and downs with finances a time or two, but they are the ups and downs of a man who is determined to make a go of it in the world without a steady stream of government "charity." Because once the government gets you hooked, it feels that it has the right to tell you what to do and how you have to live. I don't want anybody to tell me what I can or cannot do. No one *should* want that. That's for you to decide for yourself and your family. Not for me. Not for anybody else. Making those day-to-day choices is just as much what freedom means as having a position on the big, flashy issues of the day.

I got that attitude from my mother. Here's a perfect example. The little red house on Logan Street was two blocks from St. Stephen church, and though we didn't go while my father was alive, we did hear a lot about the place. At St. Stephen every year, the youth had what they called the Sunday school picnic. It started as an annual picnic on the lawn, but it got bigger and more elaborate over the years. Eventually they moved it to a local park, then to a picnic area by a lake. Finally, the Sunday school picnic got so big they decided to make it a trip to the big amusement park in Charlotte called Carowinds.

The year it moved to Carowinds, Alice and Michael got to go to the Sunday school picnic. Although we did not attend church at the time, my mom and dad heard about the trip and let them go with the group. Tony and I were too little to go, however. So my big brother and sister went to the picnic, and I was sad. But what I soon discovered was that my mom had made a picnic for Tony and me. We had it right there on the porch, with a tablecloth and a cake and all the fixin's. That memory brings tears to my eyes still. It's one of the ways I define my mom, that she did that.

My mother passed away in 2016 at eighty-eight years of age. She died of pneumonia, which was a complication of several other ailments. Her last words to me also included my wife, Yolanda. It was something she always used to tell us. This time she had an oxygen mask on. She pulled it down a bit and said, "Y'all look so good. Y'all look so good." The last thing she ever said, according to my sister Gracia (who had been her caretaker in later years and was with her to the end), was my sister Alice's name.

My mother inspired me by example. She, along with my wife, helped make me the man I am today. She left behind a great legacy that I will always cherish.

What a woman and what a life!

* * *

As I stood there in that college classroom, still leaning against the wall after explaining to the professor why I never moved, I realized that it was my difficult childhood that gave me insight. It helped me to know what was important. A mother who worked as a janitor showed me what was important. Faithful men and women at church showed me what was important. Simple picnics on the front porch, rather than in a fancy park, showed me what was important. Playing make-believe on that same porch banister, imagining I was flying a plane or steering a ship with a trash can lid, showed me what was important. Walking with my siblings downtown to Western Auto to sit and watch wrestling on the color television showed me what was important.

My "privileged" classmates thought that going to private schools, taking trips to Europe, or visiting museums were the important things. They had never awakened in the morning to see their parents beaten and bloody after a night of fighting. They had never opened the cabinet

31

only to see one thing to eat instead of a myriad of choices. They had never stayed awake in the night to kill rats in the house. As a result, they didn't know what it was to hold on to everyone else in the family because there was no one else. They didn't know what it was to rely on faith alone because there was nothing else. They didn't know what it was to dig deep within to find a solution to a problem because there was no money or influential friends to solve it. Without material goods or influential means, I learned to rely on my faith, my family, and my own God-given abilities.

I can now look back on a rather difficult childhood, fraught with domestic violence and poverty, and say that I had a fantastic childhood. I know that had my mother made a different choice after my father's death, had she listened to the well-meaning though faulty advice, had she failed to surround us with godly individuals, my values would have been shaped in a totally different way. As a young black man, I learned the importance of working to live. I learned that finding a job is possible, even when up against unbelievable odds. I learned to trust in God. I learned that being together is most important, not the house in which you live. Parents need to hear this today. The choices you make when your children are watching have the potential to build up or tear down a future attitude of perseverance. I can say without hesitation that my mother's choices solidified the conservative values I possess that have led me to this point in my life.

3

TRAINS AND SPEECHES

THE RAILROADS of Greensboro and I go way back. Trains have filled my imagination since I was a small child.

When I think about trains, I don't relate to them the way most people do. When many people see a train, they might think, "Oh, a train. Wonder where it's going." Something like that. Some people don't even see them. They don't spare them a glance. But when I see a train, I don't see a thing. I see—a personality. A train is alive to me. It's a bizarre thing. Now don't call me crazy. I'm a grown man. I know it's not *really* alive. But to this day when I have free time, I will drive down the street where I live. I will turn and head down Sandy Ridge Road, down to the train tracks. I'll stop on the tracks and look both ways to see if the train is coming. If it's not, I will turn left and go down to an area with several industries where the train pulls in and does work, where it picks up cars and drops off cars. If it's not there, I'll keep going. I'll look for the train. I'll go all the way to Kernersville for the sight of a train.

If I spot a train, I don't sit mute. I literally start talking to it, especially to the locomotive.

"There it is! I see you! You can't hide from me!"

I suppose this is the way a man might speak to his favorite dog, roughly but lovingly.

It's a combination of fascination and danger. Or the way a hunter might speak to a big bear he knows, a bear he will not even attempt to shoot but will watch go on its way. I've always had this reaction. When I was in junior high school, I would go down to the train tracks often. We lived on Dudley Street then. Dudley Street crossed over East Market. At East Market, there is a main post office, and then there's a railroad that runs behind it across Dudley Street. I would walk to that crossing. Then, if you follow that crossing all the way down, you will walk into downtown Greensboro. There's a small rail yard down there. I would walk down those train tracks, usually with a couple of buddies. The goal was to keep going until we saw the train coming. Then we would turn around and run back to the Dudley Street crossing on the tracks between the rails.

At times I would be running on the tracks with the train right behind me. I remember one time when the guy in the train was leaning out his window and screaming at me to get off the tracks. He called me some pretty choice words.

But that is far from the most dangerous thing I did around trains as a teenager.

Greensboro is a city of trains. I grew up surrounded by them. The creosote-and-steel odor seeps from the yards. Oil and grease spatter paints the gravel. Electricity crackles and sparks at the switching elements. Directional lights—green, red, bright white—flash on and off. Wrist-thick rods push and the steel point rail pivots against the hell block.

A mighty locomotive rolls by, compressing the very ground under it; the train weighs so much that it grinds the gravel against itself. The sight of a train has always filled me with a sense of danger and awe—but most of all, with a sense of familiarity. I spent hours, days, watching trains. I loved the locomotives most, as any boy would.

The trains of Greensboro were black with a white stripe. They also had a gold pinstripe on them that said "Southern." This is what train enthusiasts call the "tuxedo scheme Southern:" a black engine with a white stripe and thin gold pinstripe that said "Southern." I remember the first time I saw something besides "Southern" written on a train. It had the same tuxedo paint scheme, black with white stripe, but the gold lettering read, "Central and Georgia." This astonished me. I can remember standing at the tracks as a kid and jumping up and down and shouting, "Oh, look, it's something different!" If a Union Pacific locomotive had gone by, I probably would have had a heart attack.

I remember when I first saw a Norfolk Southern with a horse on it and was so excited. That's when I was in high school. I spotted it over on Murrow Boulevard and followed it for miles. On the model railroad I'm building now, the engines have Southern tuxedo schemes. That's why I love them. To think that I grew up all those years wanting to see a different engine, but now I want a Southern tuxedo scheme to remind me of the good old days.

I did dangerous things around trains as a boy. When I remember one activity I engaged in, the hair on the back of my neck stands up. In Greensboro, the train would stop on the tracks at times. If I wanted to cross, I would crawl underneath the train and go to the other side. One day while I was in ninth grade, almost in high school, I got a bright idea. A train was in my path. It was moving slowly, however. After a moment's hesitation, I skirted under while it was moving. I lay down flat on the track, my back as flush against the gravel as I could make it, as the train passed over me. I was surrounded by the deep rumble and the steely clanging, squeaks, and squeals of the train cars. It felt like being inside a man-made tornado. I rolled off after the last set of wheels was past.

I did it once, and when I did, it was like I had jumped from a bridge or parachuted out of an airplane. I sighed in a long "ah," as adrenaline coursed through me.

Of course, I felt compelled to do it again. And I did, several times. It goes without saying that the adult me believes this was extremely dangerous and completely stupid, to say the least. There are many cables hanging down from a train's undercarriage, for instance. Sometimes the cars have loose spring rods angled down diagonally, raking the track. Any of these could easily split a young boy from head to foot. Sometimes when a train hits a rough spot in the track, these components will break off and fly like shrapnel.

The last time I performed my "lie under a train" routine, I remember distinctly counting aloud as I was flat on my back with the train going over the top of me.

"One Mississippi, two Mississippi"

The back of one boxcar, the front of the next. The first set of wheels passed by.

"Three Mississippi, four Mississippi."

The second set rolled by, the back of the car, the coupler, the next car. "Five Mississippi."

I told myself: You have to let the second set pass by, then you roll off.

But that time, I miscounted. I started my roll early. If I'd rolled over completely, I would have rotated into that second set of wheels and been crushed.

Something told me to stop, some sixth sense about trains. That second set of wheels went by, and I finally rolled out from under. I sit here considering it now and think, "What in the world was I doing? What kind of mindset was I in?" It still makes my stomach hurt.

You'd think that would be the worst of it, but there was a time in high school when I came even closer to being run over by a train—seconds longer and I'd have been dead. We were on a JROTC drill meet. Throughout high school, I was heavily involved with drill and went to many competitions. This time the meet was at Campbell University. We were staying in Lillington, North Carolina, and while we were at the hotel that evening, a group of us saw a Domino's Pizza sign. We decided to walk over to the pizza place.

As we were walking, we came up to a train crossing. The light began to go off. Ding, ding, ding! My friends did the smart thing. They ran across the train track.

I ran across with them. But then I decided—Mr. Smartbutt, because I know trains—to go back onto the tracks. I walked back across real slow, real cool. My best friend Wayne Campbell can confirm this is a true story. My friends were shouting at me to get off the tracks. I walked along like I owned the rail line. When I got to the middle of the crossing, I turned toward the oncoming train, stood there, and watched the light approaching. I felt the rush of familiarity and danger I was so accustomed to.

"I got this. I got this," I said.

The engineer perhaps saw me. He knew it was a crossing in any case. The horn blew and blew. I judged the position of the light—and stepped off the tracks. I stepped off on the opposite side to my friends.

As soon as I stepped from the tracks—I mean, the second I was off—the train blew past me at seventy miles an hour.

I had thought it was a freight train. It was not. It was an Amtrak passenger train. Freight trains go slower, a lot slower.

If I had stood on the track another moment, I would've gotten run over. I would have been killed.

Did I recognize this in the moment? Did I feel remorse?

Of course not. The train whizzed by me. I was in shock, but also jubilant. The ground shook beneath me. My legs were wobbling, and I was about to fall on the ground. The train roared by. I could hear my friends on the other side screaming at the top of their lungs "Mark! Mark!"

That's when I got a bright idea. I thought, "They believe I got run over."

One my side of the track there was a drainage ditch. Before the entire length of the train had passed, I jumped into the ditch and hid.

Then the train was gone. I crouched in the ditch, smiling to myself. I heard the pattering feet of my JROTC buddies as they scuttled over. They were screaming and crying my name. They thought I was dead, and they expected to find a mangled body. Or maybe just a greasy patch on the ground.

That's when I popped out of the ditch.

After they got over their astonishment, it turned out that they did not think this was particularly funny. A couple of them wanted to beat me to death and were only dissuaded by Wayne Campbell. They'd all thought I was a goner.

So, for a moment, did I.

Of course now I fully understand how perilous this all was and how close I came to harming myself and bringing grief to others. Obviously I don't condone it. Yet that energy within me and the desire to take chances, once harnessed and turned to sane and proper ends, have served me well in adulthood.

* * *

Often children who have an insecure home life depend on the stability of school. Being able to go to the same place each day and interact with teachers who care and friends who cheer is a source of comfort. As an elementary-aged child, I did not have this stability. Not only were my childhood years characterized by a violent and impoverished home life, but I also attended more than a few elementary schools because of zoning changes. I went to Brooks, to Irwin, to Porter, and finally to Lindley. In fact, I never went to the school that was within walking distance of my class, Washington Street Elementary. The decisions of politicians affected me even then. Complications with desegregation were still an issue in Greensboro during the seventies. Our school system always seemed to be adjusting districts and busing students to schools in neighborhoods not their own. For example, my older siblings had attended an elementary school just around the corner from where we lived. But when I started school, the district lines had shifted, and I was bused across town. This happened at more than one school. I felt like I spent as much time on the school bus as I did in school. As a result, in elementary school, I found it difficult to make and keep friends. Just as I started to get to know a group of students and teachers, the next year would find me at a new school, starting all over again. Back then, you often heard in the media of white parents who complained about the destruction of their neighborhood schools by forced busing. I can assure you the results were not any better for black families. Segregation was ended in the 1960s, but the attempts to "fix" the education system by misguided social scientists made sure its legacy continued much further into the future than it should have. There were other sensible solutions that might have been put in place—solutions that would not end up punishing the very children the regulations were ostensibly designed to help. You don't end inequality by destroying a community and the hard-won base of wealth that sustained it, all in the name of social progress. You conserve and build on what people have already achieved instead. It's a lesson we are still learning.

In addition to feeling shuttled around, I was often picked on, today we would say bullied, for being poor. I remember, in particular, a girl from a nice middle-class community, who lived not far from my neighborhood with its poor housing. One day, she observed me in the store using food stamps to purchase some things we needed. She returned to school the next day to announce to the whole class what she had seen. In turn, many others taunted me that day for having to use food stamps. I was appalled. It wasn't so much that I felt ashamed of my own circumstances as that I was hurt by the mean and gossipy nature of the girl and some of the other children. They had all adopted a superior attitude toward me for something I could not help. That girl didn't know anything about me or my family and was making assumptions that didn't have anything to do with reality.

Not long ago I saw that same girl, now a middle-aged woman, at an event in our coliseum. I had entered the political arena by this time and was there for my campaign. She was working one of the concession stands. I had the chance to say hello to her, and she responded very pleasantly. I don't know if she thought about that day in the grocery store with the food stamps, but that memory certainly came back to me. I had to remind myself that this woman was now fully grown and probably a very different person from that little girl. But I am not perfect, and I found a bit of that childhood resentment welling up. Fortunately,

I smiled and behaved like a grown man, and it quickly dissipated. That day was another reminder to me that it's not where you come from, nor what you did or did not experience, that makes you privileged. It's your attitude toward others. Attitudes are not set in stone by some sort of inevitable social force you cannot control. Attitudes can be changed.

* * *

Thankfully, my middle and high school years would afford me the sense of stability in my educational experience that I needed. I attended Mendenhall Junior High, now Mendenhall Middle School, the first school that I attended as a student for multiple years. During those three years at the same school, I made many friends. I may have disliked the schoolwork, but I looked forward to school each day, knowing I would see that group of kids, my companions.

Back in my day, middle school in Greensboro went through ninth grade. My ninth-grade year found me in Mrs. Nancy Osborne's English class. Every year, the ninth grade students had to give a speech in their English class. The teachers would select students from their classes to present their speeches at the school-wide level. The best students from the school would be chosen to present their speeches at the city-wide level.

I knew I would have to present a speech; there was no way to get out of the assignment. My classmates began working on their speeches right away and practicing too. There were a few students who went to the library each day to rehearse their speeches. We had whole class periods with people doing this, and I thought, "This is great! I don't have to do anything this period." I was not excited about any of it and felt no pressing need to prepare for my speech.

So I procrastinated. The night before the presentation I still had not written anything, but the time had come. I told my mother I needed some notecards. So she took me to Eckerd's Drugs and bought them for me. We brought the cards home, but I still put it off.

Finally I said to myself, "Well, it's due tomorrow. You'd better write something." The theme was "service with pride." I considered this. I used to love the public service announcements that featured the cartoon dog McGruff, who was a dog detective who "took a bite out of crime." I decided I would talk about stopping crime, and how doing certain things to stop crime would be a service to the community.

So I wrote my speech that night before it was due. I didn't go over it aloud. I didn't read it over at all. I worked on it until I was fairly certain I could earn a C with what I had written, and then I went to bed.

Then came speech day. I had not practiced and did not know my speech as well as those who had spent day after day rehearsing. My turn came to present. I stood up in front of my class and gave my speech, clearly reading from my cards since I did not have anything memorized. After my presentation, to my utter surprise, my classmates around me began to applaud enthusiastically. We had to critique the speeches after they were given, and the class went around talking about what they liked, such as specific things I'd said or points I'd made. As class ended, they continued to congratulate me, saying "Wow, that was so good!"

I had not expected this response. Not at all.

At the end of class, Mrs. Osborne stopped me before I could leave the room. "How long did you practice that speech?" she asked. I wasn't sure what to reply. If I told her the truth, that I had not practiced it at all, would she then give me a bad grade, or a worse grade than the C I was hoping for? In the end, I didn't think it would be a good idea to lie to her, so I told her the truth.

"I didn't practice at all. I just wrote it last night."

She looked at me with disbelief. "There is no way you wrote that last night," she concluded. But I repeated that it was true, that I had written it the previous night and had not practiced.

"Do you realize how well you gave that speech and how good that speech really was?" she asked me. I replied with a simple "no" because I really had no idea what she was talking about.

This may seem surprising, but to this day when I get a similar response from an audience, I have a hard time believing it. Perhaps this is partly because when I am making a speech, I do not stand apart observing myself. I'm fully into what I'm saying.

I'm not sure what I did that day, but apparently it was effective. Ms. Osborne explained to me that I would be going on to present my speech at the school level. Her one note was that I needed to work on maintaining eye contact with my audience—as far as I can remember, that was her sole piece of advice—and she began working with me after school on public speaking. I did work a lot on eye contact with the audience, and I improved greatly with her help.

The day came to present my speech in front of the entire school body of Mendenhall Junior High. I remembered what Ms. Osborne had taught me and presented my improved speech. Once again, to my surprise, I received a standing ovation and was nominated to compete at the next level, for Greensboro City.

The city-level competition took place at a country club in Greensboro. My mom was able to attend, and Mrs. Osborne was there as well. I presented my speech on stopping crime, and there it was again—a standing ovation. It was a proud moment in my life. It was also baffling. I thought "Are they doing this because they pity me?"

I did not win that day. I lost to a fellow classmate.

Well, let me tell it like it is. Or was. I lost to the son of the mayor of Greensboro. Yes, his son gave a good speech. At least I thought so. But so did I, apparently.

Again, I was surprised at the reaction of the crowd afterward. When the winner was announced, there was an audible sigh from the audience, almost a groan. At least that's the way I remember it.

Afterward, Ms. Osborne came over to put her arm around me. She encouraged me not to be disappointed. I told her I was not. I really wasn't. I had made it to the city level of competition quite unexpectedly. I'd taken second place in the whole city of Greensboro. How could I be disappointed?

As I was walking out, more than one man put an arm on my shoulder then slapped me on the back and proclaimed, "That was real good. You'da won that, boy, if you hadn't been up against the mayor's son."

At home that night, my mom was telling my brothers and sisters about the speech. She was adamant that I lost to the other kid only because he was the mayor's son. Mom thought it was unfair. Maybe I did lose because I was going up against the mayor's son. Maybe not. Either way, the speech was a defining event in my life.

"You can feel it. It's his gift from God," my wife Yolanda has said of my public speaking. "Of course, I know him and may have just been talking with him about this or that. Then he gets up and . . . it can be awe-inspiring, even for me. It's still surprising."

So I didn't know where it came from then and still don't, but in ninth grade, a talent for public speaking had manifested itself quite accidentally. I will forever be grateful to Mrs. Osborne for noticing this ability in me and taking the time to help me develop it. At the end of my ninth grade year, Mrs. Osborne signed my yearbook, wishing me good luck in the future. She wrote that she was sure whatever I did in life would involve public speaking.

It did. But this was a long time coming.

4

JROTC, COWBOY BOOTS, AND PACHELBEL'S "CANON"

WHEN WE LIVED at 409 Dudley Street, North Carolina A&T University was a block away. A&T's homecoming parade used to be a big deal. Since we lived catty-corner from A&T, people were always looking for someplace to park in order to go over to the parade on campus. At that time, we had an empty lot by the house. One year, a guy pulled up in a big Lincoln. As kids, we were fascinated by cars.

We'd sit on the porch, cover up our eyes, and somebody would say, "You want the next car that comes down the road?"

"Yeah, I want that car."

You'd open your eyes, and it might be a terrible car—a Pinto or an AMC Pacer. Or, it could be a big Cadillac, and you'd be cheering, throwing your arms up in the air. "I got that car!"

So that homecoming day, the man parked his Lincoln in the lot next to us. We were eyeing it, whispering about it. We were uninhibited kids, so we asked him, "Hey mister, how much did that car cost?"

The man smiled ruefully. "I paid about $7,000 for this car," he said.

"What? Woah!"

So for a long time I used to say, "Man, one day I want to buy a car that costs $7,000."

When my wife and I were test driving her new car recently, this came back to me. Perhaps that's why, when it was my turn to drive, I unconsciously headed toward the house on Dudley Street.

We were about to drop a *whole lot* more than $7,000 on this vehicle, and it wasn't even a particularly expensive car. Times have changed.

* * *

After completing ninth grade at Mendenhall, I was to attend Grimsley High School. I was not looking forward to this; in fact, I was very angry about the move to high school. All of my friends from Mendenhall would be attending Page High School. This was going to be like elementary school all over, changing from school to school and losing all my friends. I desperately wanted to go to Page with my friends. They were the first group of school friends I had ever had for more than a year. But because of where I lived, I had to attend Grimsley.

My brother Michael, who is eight years older than I am, had attended Grimsley. There he had been heavily involved in the Marine-based JROTC program. When I was very young, I thought he was *in* the Marines. I used to go to the library and look at books about soldiers. I was very into it, and I was looking forward to participating when I got to high school.

But the program at Grimsley was defunct, or so I believed. I had greatly admired all the things Michael had learned and done with JROTC, and now I was not going to get a chance to follow in his footsteps. Then one day during my eighth grade year, when I was at the bus stop, I saw the older brother of a friend of mine wearing a green uniform. He was currently going to Grimsley. I asked my friend, Steve Burwell, about this, and he said, "Yeah, they got JROTC at Grimsley."

"Is it Marines or what?"

"It's Army now."

"Where're we going?"

"We're going to Page."

"Dang!"

Page did not have a JROTC program.

Then when I suddenly found myself assigned to Grimsley at the end of the school year, I knew there would be a JROTC program. My friends were going to Page, but this provided a faint hope that things wouldn't be all bad at Grimsley.

As it turned out, Grimsley High School and the experiences I had there would shape me for the rest of my life.

Nevertheless, I walked into the halls of Grimsley High with the proverbial chip on my shoulder, prepared to be miserable. However, after only one day, I loved Grimsley and the high school life. The Grimsley Junior Reserve Officers' Training Corps was indeed active, and I immediately joined. JROTC is a military-regulated program offered as a class at many high schools. Grimsley High had this class, and I took it, not really knowing what to expect. JROTC gave me a sense of purpose and a focus in school that, up to that time, I had not known. Also, the class helped me discover another hidden talent when I joined the drill team.

Initially, I had only wanted to be a part of the JROTC color guard, as my brother Michael had been. The color guard presented the flag at sporting events, a task I considered to be extremely important. I didn't want to be on the drill team. My perception of what they did was skewed. I imagined it to be more like a dance team. But two new friends I'd made at Grimsley forced me to go to the first drill team meeting. After that meeting, I was all in. Our instructor had been a part of the Army's drill team, The Old Guard. He taught me to do individual precision drill, and I became very good. Our drill team participated in drill competitions across the state. We won top honors in many of those competitions. In individual competition, I won first place in most of them. During my senior year, I became the commander of the drill team and color guard. I was known throughout high school for my involvement in JROTC. My participation in the JROTC program gave me my most enduring memories from Grimsley High School.

JROTC was in the education building next to the bus parking lot at Grimsley. There was a main room, the sergeant major's office, and the armory behind that, which contained our drill rifles and all our rifle team rifles. The rifle team rifles, which fired real bullets, were in a safe. The drill team rifles for the entire battalion were up on racks.

My family came to see me when I was in the color guard, and my mother saw me practice. The competitions were always out of town, and my family couldn't attend, but they were supportive. I was not the only one with military ambitions in my family. By this time, my sister Alice had joined the Marines. She was stationed in California and then Japan. She spent four years as a Marine. Michael did not end up joining after his Marine-based JROTC, and Tony was never tempted by the armed forces. He believed the military would be too much like *Gomer Pyle*, which he and I had watched religiously in reruns.

I've sometimes thought that if it hadn't been for Army JROTC, if somebody today asked me what high school I went to, I might have to think about it a moment before answering. But being on the Grimsley JROTC drill team, traveling to competitions, and presenting the colors are moments I will never forget.

JROTC didn't just give me an outlet to display my rifle-spinning talents; it also gave me direction for life beyond high school. My patriotic fervor was ignited during this time, and I dreamed that after high school I would enter the armed forces. Like my JROTC friends, I wanted to join the Army and become, well, a guy like Rambo. By this point, we had cable at home, including HBO. I watched television with all my siblings, but my brother Tony and I had a particular love for feature films. We were crazy about *First Blood* and its sequel.

I liked studying army history and practices in particular, but I had always been fascinated by the military. I enjoyed learning about military history, firepower, equipment, and tradition. I hoped to join the infantry and wanted nothing more than to end up in combat one day. I know that sounds crazy to many people, but at the time my greatest desire was to be a soldier and fight for my country. In high school, specifically through JROTC, I became more aware of how the military worked. I knew the commitment required and the grueling expectations. This did not turn me away from my dream of becoming a soldier. I made my decision to serve in the armed forces once I graduated.

I didn't play sports at all in high school. I tried out for football one time, but that didn't work out. So I concentrated on JROTC and orchestra—more on that in a moment—as my extracurriculars.

High school was a big deal for me. I was seriously engaged in the community there. My classmates often remember me from high school. I stuck out like a sore thumb. One reason for this is that I was either dressed "weird" or I had on my ROTC uniform. I was an odd dresser. Sometimes I wore parachute pants and high-top Adidas. But most of the time I was wearing cowboy boots. I was a fanatic about them. When I got my first Army reserve paycheck, the first thing I bought was a serious pair of cowboy boots. This was during my senior year in high school. By that time, cowboy boots were all I wore to school other than my uniform shoes.

Why did I love cowboy boots so much? I grew up watching Westerns. I particularly loved that half-Western, half-science-fiction show *The Wild, Wild West.* I thought Jim West was the coolest man alive. These days, my favorite Western show is *Gunsmoke.* I watch the reruns as my relaxation.

Not only did we watch people park cars next to our house on Dudley and walk over to the parade, my brothers, sisters, and I used to attend the NC A&T homecoming parade ourselves every year. There was always a contingent of Buffalo Soldiers, black men reenacting those Western cavalry units, and I would stand in awe of them as they passed by in their blue uniforms with yellow stripes down the pants. They rode horses and wore the big hats and carried those flowing cavalry flags. Impressive! You could've bought me for a nickel. I was screaming and cheering them on. I was the kind of kid who wasn't normally animated like that, but this was something that really tripped my trigger. When I watched them, it seemed the greatest thing I'd ever seen in my life. They were on those prancing horses, riding them through the streets. Henry repeating rifles flapped in their scabbards against the saddles, and the men wore great big Teddy Roosevelt revolvers on their hips.

I thought, "When I grow up, I want to be like that!"

That's why I bought that good pair of cowboy boots.

Over the years, I've had a couple of pairs of cowboy boots with soles that I wore holes in. When I was in San Antonio, training with the Army, I got my two favorite pairs of cowboy boots ever, a pair of Laredos and a pair of Naconas. I had resoled the Naconas. Years later, I had them in my old Camaro, and for some reason, I didn't lock the back. Somebody stole them, along with a Walkman and a gym bag. The only thing I was concerned about was the boots. I still have cowboy boots, but my feet have gotten fat and wide. These days, I'm a big man with big feet, and it's hard to find boots that will fit me. But I know they make them for hefty men with hefty feet, and I'm planning to get a couple of pairs by-and-by.

I thought of myself as a snappy dresser back then. What I usually had on was a pair of jeans, brown cowboy boots with gold tips on the toes, a polo shirt or a button-down shirt, and a blue blazer with brass buttons. And I had the sleeves rolled up on the blazer, of course. This was the 1980s, after all. The blue blazer thing? That caught on at Grimsley. Other people started wearing them and rolling up the sleeves.

But what people really remember me for the most from high school is JROTC—especially my ROTC uniform. I'm not blowing my own horn here, just telling the truth: when I wore that ROTC uniform— don't bump into me because I was sharp. Brass shined. Shoes gleamed. I wore that uniform every Thursday.

Each class level was its own platoon, and the platoons made up our battalion. Each platoon had its uniforms inspected on Thursday. Ribbons stacked up on my chest over time. Cords dangled over my arms. And we wore berets. The color guard wore red berets, and the drill team wore black berets. If you were in both, as I was, you wore the black beret with a red tab with your rank on it. We would cut the lining from the berets and press them to get them to lie down on the side and have the brim popped up smartly. We were a sharp unit.

Since I enjoyed JROTC so much, some have asked why I did not make a career of the Army. After all, I had already joined the real Army by the time I graduated from high school. What I didn't like about the Army, or rather what made me unsuited for the Army long term, was pretty simple. In the Army, I couldn't do what I wanted to do. I know that may sound like pride or hubris. After all, you might say that's what the Army *does*; it gives *you* orders! But there was so much I would see in the Army—methods of doing things, ways of behaving—and I could imagine a better way, a more efficient way, to do these things, and I knew I would have to spend years being told that I had to do this or that in a specific way when I knew there was a superior technique, a better method.

I did spend almost seven years in the Army. I don't regret that in the slightest! It is a great career choice for those who were made for it, and I have nothing but respect and gratitude for our service members and veterans. But I knew, and God knew, that I was not supposed to be in the Army for the rest of my working life. I think if I'd remained, I would have been very unhappy and perhaps gotten myself killed or would have taken to drinking. My realization that I was unsuited to a military career was very disappointing at the time, but I made the right decision, and I now don't regret it at all.

Yet JROTC was exactly what I needed to help me stay engaged in high school. This may sound counterintuitive, but JROTC gave me an outlet for artistic expression. What I was doing mostly was drill team. That's total creativity. It's a performance. Plus, I basically designed the uniform I drilled in. Even though we were a military-based unit, it was us, the guys who were in it, who got to decide many of the specifics of our uniforms. We got to decide how our unit was structured and how efficient we were. We had almost total control. The Army is not like that; let me assure you! But we'll get to that.

* * *

I had started playing the violin in the Porter Elementary School orchestra in fifth grade, the year my father died. But it wasn't until we moved from Logan Street to Dudley Street that I mentally moved into a wider world where music became as essential to me as breathing. Life was much more stable on Dudley Street. I joined the Mendenhall Junior High School orchestra and then the orchestra at Grimsley High School.

Back in fifth grade at Porter, I had desperately wanted to play the drums. I went to the meeting about joining the band, and they gave us a form. Then I saw that there was a list of places to go to get your instrument. My heart sank.

I went up after the presentation and asked, "So we have to *pay* for these instruments?"

Yes, we were expected to do so. I knew that wasn't going to work out. My family didn't have enough money.

I felt dejected and was getting ready to leave when my friend LaMont James said to me, "Hey, my mama can't buy me no instrument for the band either. But they are giving out free instruments over in the orchestra!"

This was a different group from the band. We went to check out the orchestra, and I found that LaMont was right. He got a viola—and I got a violin. I took it home and started sawing. I had a knack. It did not take long until learned to play by ear.

Then came the real orchestra days of junior high and high school. The days of the orchestra concert had arrived, and I lived for them.

Here's something I don't necessarily talk about a lot: I've always liked women. I was never one of those little boys who go through a phase when they don't like girls. And I didn't just like girls; I tended to fall in love with "older women," that is, adults. My orchestra teacher was practically the archetype of this for me. I was in love with that woman! All three years I was at Mendenhall, I couldn't wait to get back to school to see her. She was a petite blonde woman, perhaps not objectively beautiful. But, oh man, I was devoted to her.

I used to come home and put on that Neal Diamond song "Love on the Rocks" and think about her. Today this memory to me is as cheesy and cringy as it sounds—but, let me tell you, not back then!

Junior high school was when I started to feel I was part of something bigger than myself, a place where I could accomplish things and see my own progress. At school, I wasn't an outsider looking in. Orchestra gave me a skill that set me apart. People would see me with a violin and ask me if I could play it—and I could! I'd open the case up and start playing, and they would be impressed.

I played in the orchestra all three years at Grimsley High School. I could have been truly excellent at it if I had learned one thing: how to read music. To this day, despite all the musical experiences in my life, I still don't know how.

So how did I play the violin? I would get a piece of music assigned by the orchestra teacher, and I would go to the library and find a recording. If I couldn't find it there, I would go to a used record store in downtown Greensboro, a place that was also a bookstore. If I couldn't find the music there, I'd go to the new record store and either buy it or order it. Then I'd take it home and listen to it many times over. I would then sit down with the violin and work out how to play the piece.

There were entire works of music I broke down and memorized this way. One of my favorite pieces was Pachelbel's "Canon." I learned how to play it by ear. I learned Pachelbel's "Canon" as a mishmash of all the parts. Once my teacher heard me performing it the way I'd taught myself, she asked, "How in the world are you playing that song like that?"

I told her, "That's the way I hear it inside my head."

I was afraid she was going to ask me if I knew how to read music, so I didn't elaborate. Eventually I would learn to listen to the music, work out the parts, and memorize what I needed. I usually picked out the violin parts, but for some pieces I learned all the instrumental parts. "Clair de lune" by Claude Debussy is an example of this. It's usually a piano piece, but I figured out how to transfer it to violin. Also Rossini's "William Tell Overture." I could play all the parts to that one.

So I learned how to play music the way it sounded to me. I was in the second violin section, third chair, because I didn't read music. If I'd learned how to read music, I probably would have been second or third chair first violin, or first chair second violin all the time.

I had to learn entire works of music in this way for tryouts because the orchestra teacher would pick certain sections of the music at random for the audition. I suspect she knew I couldn't read music. Yet I was an excellent player, and she wanted the orchestra to sound good. I practiced violin all the time. Upstairs in my room on Dudley Street, I'd sit at the end of the bed and look at the music as I practiced. Of course I wasn't totally musically illiterate. I knew what a whole note was, what a half note was, and many other things about musical notations. I could identify where I was in the music as I played it. But if somebody handed me a piece of music and I hadn't heard it, I couldn't play it. I do the same thing as a singer, which is where my musical direction lies these days. I have to hear a song and commit it to memory first.

Orchestra was great. It was a wonderful experience from fifth grade to twelfth. High school concerts were the most fun of all. One year, we played a concert featuring Harold Hanson's "Song of Democracy."

Sail, Sail thy best, ship of Democracy

Of value is thy freight, 'tis not the present only

The Past is also stored in thee

We did it as a combined group: the orchestra, the band, and a choir, which was mixture of community members, students, and teachers. It was awe inspiring and beautiful.

I continued to play for a few years after high school. I performed in a big orchestra production of "Battle Hymn of the Republic" at the Shiloh Baptist Church in Greensboro. I played a couple of times at St. Stephen for Youth Day and events like that. But eventually I let the violin go. By the time I met Yolanda, I wasn't playing. She's never heard me play the violin. In fact, I've never owned a violin. It was always either a school instrument or one that I borrowed. For example, the violin on which I played "The Battle Hymn of the Republic" concert belonged to Collin Scott, my very first orchestra teacher from back at Porter Elementary, who had invited me to play at Shiloh Baptist Church that Sunday many years later.

Music and JROTC gave me direction that carried over into all my other activities as a teenager. A stable school with sound programs provided not only a safe haven for a kid like me, but a place to find myself and discover and develop skills I would later use as an adult. That is one reason I feel the need to fight to maintain the traditional structure of the great American high school and not see learning and character-forming activities dissipated by divisive social justice initiatives and activist classrooms where little real teaching occurs. For me, the fight is personal.

5

MEN OF THE RING

NOW I MUST take a detour. I have to mention an extremely important, perhaps crucial, part of my formative years, but this is difficult to do without raising an eyebrow or two on the faces of the uninitiated. To this day, it remains the most real "unreal" thing I've ever experienced—and I'm in political office!

I'm talking, of course, about professional wrestling.

At first, we watched wrestling on television—hours and hours of it. Before my mother's job and the glorious advent of cable television in our home, the usual wrestling channel was one of those you had to carefully position the antenna to receive. This big antenna was outside the house, and turning it just right to get the channel was not an easy task for a kid in grammar school. But we perfected the art, let me tell you.

"World Championship Wrestling featuring the superstars of professional wrestling!" the television would announce. Then you would hear a list of the stars. I remember them well! It might be a card like this: "Mil Mascaras, Ivan Koloff, the Mongols, Ernie Ladd, the Mighty Igor, Thunderbolt Patterson, Argentina Apollo and Luis Martino!"

My dad and my mom both *loved* professional wrestling. Wrestling was always on at our house every Saturday. And when it started coming on Sundays, we were tuned in as well.

We didn't just watch wrestling; we lived it. It became part of the way my family viewed the world, practically a secret language we shared. And when I was old enough, I began to attend the matches in person. This was back when wrestling was regional, and the stars on television could be seen in a match at the Greensboro Coliseum. We went to many of these, Alice, Michael, Tony, and me in particular. We would walk from the house to the coliseum.

The first time I went to wrestling live, I remember walking into that vast (to me) space and looking at that blue ring with NWA on the side—and I was so excited. Nothing like it.

When we were kids on Logan Street, our favorites were the Mighty Igor, Dusty Rhodes, and Bruno Sammartino. My dad's favorite wrestler was Johnny Weaver, while my mom's favorite was Jack Brisco. She adored him and thought him very handsome. Then we got older and more sophisticated and finally had color television, so our allegiances evolved. My favorite wrestlers to this day are the tag team called the Road Warriors. They used to dress in the postapocalyptic outfits like the characters in the Mel Gibson movie. They were consummate showmen. Had it all. Even today, when I am relaxing after a long day in the North Carolina Assembly or after committee meetings, I watch them in reruns online. You have to understand that this is an art form we're talking about! I love the Road Warriors. The only other wrestling act that comes close—but only close—is Goldberg. (His full name is Bill Goldberg, but he usually just went by his last name, which was a household name in any house where wrestling was venerated, such as ours. He was Jewish in real life, proclaimed it proudly, and refused to wrestle on Yom Kippur).

The Road Warriors were Road Warrior Hawk, whose real name was Michael Hegstrand, and Road Warrior Animal, whose name was Joseph Laurinaitis. Both of them were originally out of Minneapolis. They were also known as the Legion of Doom. Sadly, Road Warrior Hawk passed away in 2003, and Animal died in 2020, so the Road Warriors are no more. But they lit up the ring when they were around. They had many famous moves, but their signature move was the one they invented called the Doomsday Device. This was when one of the Road Warriors would hoist a groggy opponent onto his shoulders and the other would climb the turnbuckle or a ladder and then launch out and take the opponent all the way down to the rink floor with a clothesline arm to the neck.

Amazing! And their opponents who sold it so well were equally wonderful.

They were the total package. Big men, but they could move. A lot of those big men couldn't wrestle. I'll give you a perfect example: Ivan Putski. As the great Ernie Ladd once said, "Putski was a musclehead. He stayed up all night one time studying for a blood test."

The Road Warriors were big. They could move. They used to come into the ring to the song "Iron Man" by Black Sabbath. They would basically run to the ring, dive under the ropes, and start beating the crap out of their opponents—then they usually threw them out of the ring and dared them to get back in. And on top of that, they would come outside the ring and—especially Hawk—would talk junk with the best of them. The big men in wrestling were often horrible on the mic, but not the Road Warriors. They had great microphone skills. And they wore the face paint and the chaps. They were the whole package—superstars. They're still internationally famous. In Japan, there are arenas where matches of the Road Warriors are shown on video, and people pay to get in to see these films. They have life-sized statues of Hawk and Animal, and people still take pictures with them.

Everybody today in pro wrestling is chasing what they started. They might not like to admit it, but it's true. I'm afraid they'll never catch that magic again, not the way wrestling is going.

Of course, there was also Ric Flair, the Blackjack Mulligan, and all the rest. We watched them all. Michael and I read the memoirs of old wrestlers when they come out. It's a lifelong passion for my brother and me.

Ric Flair was maybe the most famous wrestler of my youth. The best thing about Ric Flair was his mouth, and the way he could sell a hit. He could make it look like a freight train had run into him! He did well back in the day when wrestling was localized, but if he were starting out today, he'd be a megastar. That was the '70s. Just about all of those wrestlers are gone now, passed away. It was a hard lifestyle, and it took its toll on them.

We also watched a great deal of roller derby, but I never got into that as much. As a family, we didn't watch many other sports. We disliked baseball, for example, because it would always preempt wrestling.

When you think about it seriously, our code of beliefs can be observed in how we saw wrestling. It always had an underlying morality, that sense of right and wrong. Justice, even. We didn't like the bad guys. We used to say, "The good guys went to real church, the bad guys went to the church of 'what's happening now.'" We couldn't stand to see somebody get ganged up on. The storylines were practically biblical.

And it filled our family language. The best house in our neighborhood, for instance, we called "Bruno Sammartino." Ric Flair? Well he was one of the flashy but bad cars—a tricked up Volkswagen or something. Everything was like that. We would analyze all entertainment, television shows, any kind of presentation, the way we analyzed wrestling. It was a question of right and wrong, a question of what was fair. If somebody would cheat and win the belt, then run out of the ring with it, we'd be practically shouting, "That's wrong!" I don't know if this was because that was the way we were as a family and so were drawn to wrestling and what it was about, or if we took this from wrestling. Maybe a little bit of both. The wrestlers call this creation and maintenance of the illusion "kayfabe." When we were kids, the kayfabe was what mattered to us. And it still does. Michael Hegstrand and Joseph Laurinaitis may have passed on, but I like to think they are still pulling out the Doomsday Device on their opponents in that great ring in the sky!

These days, I consider professional wrestling unwatchable because the kayfabe is all about yelling and mere rivalries. In the old days, the smack talk and vilification were a means to an end, which was the story, the morality play, that was being acted out in front of us. There was good and there was evil. Sometimes evil seemed to triumph over good, but good would always come back and whoop evil's butt. The wrestlers themselves switched out of hero and "heel" roles in a perpetual soap opera that all true fans followed closely. I cheered the good guys and booed the villains with all my heart.

Wrestling is indeed a show, but it is a show that takes supreme skill to pull off. People sometimes complain about the fake blood, but the blood is actually about the most real thing in wrestling. The practice is called "juicing." Especially in the old days, those wrestlers would cut their foreheads with razors before the match and smear on Vaseline to keep the wound from opening—until a strategic blow was struck during the match. And then the blood, real blood, flowed freely.

Rocky Johnson was one of the best wrestlers of all time. He was a black wrestler when wrestling was, shall we say, fairly white. The NWA had a plan to bring Rocky Johnson down from the WWF and make him the world champion. As the story goes, many of the wrestlers had a fit. A lot of these guys were stone-cold rednecks. And so they had to scrap those plans. There was time during that period when Ric Flair was on television, and I remember his saying something like, "They talk about bringing Rocky Johnson down here . . . the only thing Rocky Johnson can do for me is carry my bags."

Now Ric Flair was the top dog around North Carolina and the South. Years later, I was in Greensboro Coliseum, and he came in with his music and everything for a match with Johnson.

But he was wrestling not Rocky Johnson, but the Rock himself.

You know who the Rock is? Duane Johnson? Even people who know nothing about wrestling know who the Rock is. Well, the Rock came out, and the crowd went crazy. And Ric Flair and the Rock wrestled, and the Rock beat Flair. I was thinking to myself, "Boy, the tables sure have turned."

You see, the Rock's father happens to be a wrestler too. His father *is* Rocky Johnson. Now the son of Rocky Johnson is the biggest thing wrestling's ever seen. Of course, there were plenty of black wrestlers back in the day: Bo-Bo Brazil, Rufus Jones, Junkyard Dog, Thunderbolt Patterson. But none of them became world champion. To be fair, not a lot of people became world champion. The belt didn't get passed around like candy as it is now. You had to be a certain kind of wrestler to become world champion.

That all changed with Hulk Hogan and Ric Flair. That's when the belt started going to popular, showy, big-mouthed wrestlers. Back then, the champion wasn't a popular, flashy guy. He was the guy who was known as the best wrestler, somebody like Bruno Sammartino. He wasn't an over-the-top ostentatious guy doing a schtick. He was presented as a good guy. The lines now are blurred between "heel" and "face," but back then it was a very hard line. Baby-faced guys like Bruno Sammartino or Bernard Backlund were the good guys. They were plain guys, scientific wrestlers, always talking very politely. The bad guys were jerks: guys like Ernie Ladd, who was just a vile insulter, coming out calling Indians drunkards, stuff like that. If you ever watch any Ernie Ladd interviews, you'll be shocked. Wrestling was a morality play, and the good guys won in the end.

6

THE ARMY WAY

HIGH SCHOOL was a great period in my life. I made lifelong friends and learned so much about myself. Thanks to help from one of my mentors at church, I had learned to stand up for myself when I was being picked on, so bullying was no longer a major issue for me. At home, my mom had always told me I could be anything I wanted to be. This was a recurring theme in my home, but sometimes I had a hard time believing it as a child. However, during high school I met people—teachers and other adults—who told me that they had come from a poor family too. Some told me they had lived with an alcoholic father or a drug-addicted mother. Others had a variety of challenging circumstances, and yet here they were, successful. My eyes began to open to the fact that being poor and closed off from high society was the shell I had come from, but not where I had to stay. There were opportunities in the world that were open even to someone like me, and these successful adults were proof of that. I began to realize that everything my mom had told me was true. I began to believe that I really could be whatever I wanted to be.

And I wanted to be a soldier.

Now, my plan was to join the military and be full-time right away. But so many people told me, "You should go to college first." I was a bit confused, thinking each plan was important and worthwhile, but I could not do both at once. Then I had someone approach me to say "Yes, you can." I discovered that I could enter the reserves and attend college at the same time. The best part was finding out that the Army would pay for me to attend college. Once I had that knowledge, my thinking began to shift. I still desperately wanted to join the infantry. My dream had not changed. But there were other factors involved. I wanted to do something to make my mom proud and at the same time earn some money and help lift some financial burdens from her shoulders. So as a high-school teenager, I decided to join the reserves and began attending reserve drills during my senior year. My plan was to serve in the reserves and attend college at the same time.

I graduated high school and went straight to Fort Bliss, Texas, for eight weeks of basic training. It was June of 1986, it was hot, and the sun was strong. Allow me to say that although many people think a black man's skin will not burn in the sun, I can testify otherwise. Basic training was not easy. My life was, for the most part, on lockdown and controlled minute by minute for the entirety of those weeks. If you had to be somewhere and did not show up on time, someone would find you. There was no side-stepping the rules, expectations, or regulations. The daily regimen was a strict but necessary one. Basic training for the Army at Fort Bliss gave me an appreciation for freedom. In fact, I believe one of the byproducts of the design of basic training is to help you realize the blessing of freedom and living as free men.

Fort Bliss, practically in El Paso, Texas, was about as different from Greensboro, North Carolina as you can get. I've mentioned how strange the geography seemed to me. I was away from my home and family for the first time. I'd taken my first airplane ride ever to get out to Texas. My biggest takeaway from basic was the sense that I was getting things done.

I have heard it said that a military man does more before six a.m.

than most people do all day. It's true. We were up before the sun, out on the road. We would jog and sweat and then return to shower, make our beds, and clean up the barracks. Breakfast was served promptly, and just as we'd finished eating and were taking our plates to the sink, the sun would come up. I must say, this left me with a great feeling of accomplishment. It was satisfying to complete so much before daybreak.

After basic training, I went on to advanced individual training at Fort Sam Houston near San Antonio, Texas. This was the hands-on training for the specific Army reserve job that I would perform. I was trained as a 91A10 Medical Specialist. This certified me to work in a military hospital setting as a nurse's aide or in the field as a medic in combat situations. My training time at Fort Sam Houston gave me more freedom than I had at Fort Bliss. I discovered a new sense of wonder at being on my own. I was just out of high school and in the big city of San Antonio. I no longer felt like the kid from a ramshackle house on Logan Street. I was a young man, a soldier, walking through the streets with my head held high and my chest out square. I went from never having earned money to earning what was a lot of money in my eyes. People would look at me as I walked by in my uniform, knowing that I was serving my country. I felt a sense of accomplishment. I was doing something. The world was opening up to me. I saw things I had never seen before, things I never imagined I would see. There were large hotels, the Riverwalk, and the Alamo. I thought to myself, "I can do anything now."

I learned the structured life necessary to serve in the military. While my civilian friends were walking to class or driving to work, I was jogging in mass formation in the early hours of the morning and learning how to save soldiers' lives in combat. I will remember my time in the Army as one of the best of my life. I was able to meet interesting people, experience different things, and see parts of this country that I may never have visited otherwise.

When my training at Fort Sam Houston was complete, I returned home to North Carolina. I was attached to the United States Army Reserve 396th Ambulance Company in Winston-Salem. As such, I would be required to report, in uniform, for reserve drills one weekend every month and for one full week each year.

* * *

After returning home, I was eager to begin the next step in my life's pursuit—starting college. I enrolled at NC A&T University and planned to major in communications. Things could not have been falling into place any better. I had joined the reserves and successfully finished basic and advanced training, I was earning money as a reserve medic, and I was about to embark on the journey to obtain a college degree. In my eyes, the world was my oyster. I felt like I could do anything.

Then, as has happened to many a young man, I came up against my own limitations in a hard way. I was trying to do too much too fast.

I quickly realized, once I began my first semester at A&T, that college was not then the place for me. Earning a degree had seemed like a good idea, but I was not focused enough to be in the college classroom at that time in my life. Most people would assume that my time training for the Army reserves would have given me the solid, disciplined foundation a young man needed to do well in college. However, the discipline required at the university was different. At college, nobody tells you what to do or keeps track of your every step along the way. It is interesting to reflect how the independence of studying on my own, going to school, and engaging in scholarship, which would so energize me in later years, at that time felt like running into a brick wall.

I did not have a grasp of the process and commitment necessary to do well in my classes. I didn't understand how to make the best use of the help the university offered to keep me on track. I was not mentally prepared for the fact that the professor would hand out an assignment and not give constant reminders of its due date. I didn't know how to handle the freedom of choosing to go to class or not. No one was going to call home to Mom if I didn't go to class. No drill sergeant was going to give me push-ups. The decisions, and consequences, were on me. I was simply not ready. On top of that, I had become far more interested in chasing pretty girls than learning anything in a classroom. In the end, I dropped out after only one semester.

However, looking back, I see that God used even that brief time as a freshman at NC A&T for his purposes. Wayne Campbell, who remained my best friend after high school, invited me to attend Evangel Fellowship, a church he attended that also had on-campus activities. Although I had attended church for as long as I can remember, I had never truly heard about the need for salvation, or at least I had never understood it. I heard the gospel message at Evangel Fellowship and understood for the first time the need to respond to and follow Jesus. I knew I needed salvation. I knew that the things I had been doing were sinful, and I needed to give them up. I accepted Jesus Christ as my savior at that time. I did not, however, experience a drastic conversion like some do. My behavior did not immediately reform. They say sin is fun for a season, and I was in that season. I didn't want to give up that lifestyle, and internally I fought not to.

I would see my friend Wayne coming toward me and would cringe, wishing I could get away from him because I knew he would call me out on what I was doing (which was partying too much and toying with women with no intention of getting serious). But Wayne was a true and patient friend to me. Even today I know I could call Wayne, and he would be there for me. I am most grateful, though, that God is patient in the process of sanctification, in growing and maturing us as believers. I couldn't see that then, as a wild college freshman, but I know it now as an adult.

After that brief semester when I found out I was not ready for college, I wondered what to do. I was living at home. Some would think that my mom would have been upset and disappointed that I had dropped out of college. However, that was not really the case. While I know she wanted what was best for me, she probably knew I wasn't ready. She was most concerned that I would be a productive member of society who worked and stayed out of trouble. I got a job delivering pizzas, and I signed up for a three-year commitment to the Army reserves. So

I worked and continued my reserve drills monthly. I did not see combat or become the Rambo figure about whom I had dreamed. I was a medic in the reserves during peacetime. This is not to say I never had anything do! I did make use of those skills.

When I was in the Army, I discovered that it was not the place for me long-term. It just didn't fit my personality type. I asked too many questions aloud and wanted to know "why" too much. I loved it when I first joined, and I believe it helped me grow up and find the person I wanted to become. I had joined in the reserve and was planning to go into the active Army, but after three years in the reserve, I went to my recruiter and said, "I don't want to do this." So I transferred to the individual ready reserve, where I finished up my service. I thought I might get called back during Desert Storm, but I didn't. People sometimes ask me what I did in the Army, and I tell them I was a "backup joke teller." I used to drive around putting bandages on, smoking cigarettes, and watching people jump out of airplanes and sometimes break their legs. I certainly did nothing in comparison to some of these guys who have deployed. I have a buddy now who did two combat tours in Afghanistan.

But I *was* a 91A10, and I did my duty splinting broken legs from those parachute landings as well as tending to the usual cuts, sprains, and bruises.

There was one incident when a couple of soldiers were digging a trench. This was a basic training course running with reserve sergeants at Fort Bragg. A kid had anaphylactic shock during the course, and they had taken him to the hospital. Everyone was ordered to stop working until the medic got back. But these two geniuses digging a trench with trenching tools decided they would keep going. One of the boys was down in the trench, digging. They ran into a root. As you may know, a trenching tool, is sharp on one edge. The other fellow swung down to cut the root and it glanced off the root's surface. The other boy was bent over, and the trenching tool on its rebound sliced right along the top of his skull, practically scalping him.

When I got there, it was dark, and I shined a flashlight on him. He was sitting on the edge of the trench saying, "Is it bad? Is it bad?"

There was blood running down his face, and his hair was sticking up at a very wrong angle. I could see the bottom of his scalp exposed. I could literally see his skull. He was lucky he didn't lose any brain cells or get hit in the face and have an eye put out.

I said, "Oh no, you're fine, you're good. You might end up a little baldheaded after a while, but you're going to be okay."

I poured some sterile water on it and some Betadine, put a bandage on it, and wrapped it up for a trip to the hospital, then away he went.

* * *

I had joined the Army reserve the summer between my junior and senior year in high school. I knew what I wanted to do, after all, so I went down to the recruiting office and made the commitment. While I was in the twelfth grade, I was already attached to my reserve unit, the 396th Ambulance Company in Winston-Salem. Every weekend of the month I went to a reserve drill at the 396th. I did not have a uniform at that time, but I went to the drill, got in formation, and these guys would show me around. Even better, I got paid every month!

So I was in the Army reserve my senior year of high school. After I graduated from my medic AIT training at Fort Sam Houston, I had returned to Greensboro and into my old reserve unit. Now I had my own uniform, and I was an official crew member of the outfit. I got assigned an ambulance. We would drill one weekend a month, with annual training once a year. We went to Texas one year, Fort Benning one year, Fort Bragg another. I did about three years in the active reserve. During that time, I signed up to join the active Army. There was a long period between signing up and the time I was supposed to leave. During that period, I was working at the pizza restaurant. Soon I was a manager trainee there, making pretty good money.

I realized I did not want to go in the Army. My reasons were complicated. Some of them were banal. I wanted to stay in the workforce and keep making a civilian paycheck. I was too much of a talker and didn't want to always keep my opinions to myself. Some were more serious. I wasn't suited for the Army and didn't want to be a disappointment to the Army or myself. I was getting married. I was soon to have a child. But it was the right decision, and I've never regretted it.

I called my recruiter and told him, "I don't want to go. I just want to stay with my reserve unit."

He said, "Well, no, you have to go."

And I replied, "I'm coming up on seven years in the reserves. I like it there. I cannot be made to go in the active Army if I don't want to."

He came to see me. I told him I wanted to remain in the reserve only.

By that time, he saw I was serious and let up a little.

"I'll see, but I don't think you are going to be able to do that."

About a week or two later, I got a letter that said I'd been placed in the individual ready reserve (IRR). If I wasn't going to join the active US Army, I couldn't go back to my regular unit.

I was disappointed—I enjoyed the reserve and the 396th—but I finished up my military service in the IRR. This meant I didn't get paid. I also didn't have to go to drill. I was still in the reserves. If my reserve unit got called to war, I was going. And that was it. I served six years and change total, and about two years of that time was IRR time.

I finished out my time, got an honorable discharge, and was out of the Army. Little did I know it, but I was soon to enter civilian life full-bore. I was about to get married and have a son.

I did return to college many years later. In fact, I did an oral history project there in which I interviewed Vietnam veterans. They were black Vietnam veterans, people I'd known all my life. I picked several individuals. One was my JROTC instructor, Laizel Freeh. I spoke with Karl Hayes from church. Karl knew me from the time I was a little kid, as did Joe Andrews, who was my sister-in-law's father. When I talked to Karl, he spoke to me like I was a kid. But he was saying things such as "You probably never heard of that; you probably weren't around." Same thing with Laizel Freeh. But *he* was talking as if I were still a high school student. Those who knew me as an adult spoke of far more adult matters from Vietnam. This was practically a microcosm of my own developing maturity while serving in the Army. Even though I did not become a career military man, the military helped form my character. In many ways, it proved the perfect way to transition to manhood.

Serving in the military gave me a sense of pride and a feeling of competence for sure, and I will never regret my time there. But of course, even a healthy sense of pride can easily turn into arrogance.

7

ONE NIGHT IN RAMSEUR

SURE ENOUGH, my early years as an adult proved to be ones of arrogance and self-centeredness. I spent the years after high school earning a living by delivering pizzas and earning muscles by going to the gym. I was no longer the small kid being bullied. I was in the Army reserves. I had grown tall and muscular. I found myself wishing someone would say the wrong things to me so that I could punch their lights out, just to show that I could do it. My free time was reserved for chasing women. At this time, I had the wrong view about women and was the stereotypical jerk looking for only one thing. I knew it was a sinful pursuit, and the life of sowing wild oats was truly unfulfilling. I knew there was more to life than what I was living day to day, but I lacked the motivation to pursue anything different.

There were some nice women in my life that I wanted to get to know better. But whenever I would find myself near one, I—who was famously never at a loss for words—just couldn't seem to find the right ones. It wasn't a matter of being articulate. It was a matter of self-esteem. I seemed to have no trouble talking to the women who were bad for me, or more accurately, women who were living a lifestyle similar to mine. I think I believed that a woman worth a long-term investment would not be interested in a man like me.

As it often goes, I was not necessarily searching for a wife when I first met the woman who would become mine.

My friend Anthony Spearman was still in high school when we started hanging out together. His sister's name was Lynn. She was one year ahead of me in high school. One evening early in 1989, Anthony and I wanted to borrow Lynn's car. She said if we wanted to borrow her car, we had to take her to Ramseur, North Carolina. Ramseur is a small town south of Greensboro, between Asheboro and Siler City.

Little did I know that the little town of Ramseur would become a very large part of my life in the next few years.

Anthony and I agreed to take her. Neither one of us had a car, and we had places we wanted to *go* that night, so we drove Lynn to see her boyfriend, Roger. But when we arrived, Lynn wouldn't let us just drive away. No, she made us come inside so she could introduce us to everyone.

Lynn Spearman had been telling her friend Yolanda Hill about me, and she wanted Yolanda to get a look in person. She had an intuition that we might hit it off.

I entered the house and walked toward the den, where I saw a lady seated on a four-poster stool at her aunt's kitchen bar. I was immediately taken and thought to myself "Who is that *woman*?"

That's how she seemed to me. Not some girl, but a grown woman.

She's a little over three months older than I am, but she appeared to be a well-dressed, grown lady; her hair was nicely styled. I thought she seemed like a schoolteacher or businesswoman or at least *something* elevated. At the time, I felt that I was just a stupid kid hanging out and being stupid. From her dress and demeanor, I sensed she was a high-class woman, together, mature. She was someone who would not give me the time of day.

"She won't want to go out with me, won't want anything to do with me," I thought.

That turned out not to be the case, thank the Lord.

Like I have said, I was coming off a dumb portion of my early life. But at first, my instinct seemed to be true. After exchanging greetings, Yolanda and I didn't talk that night.

But over the next week, Lynn persisted. She set up a date. It was, in some ways, the only date Yolanda and I ever had.

We went to see *Bill and Ted's Excellent Adventure*. We've been together ever since.

* * *

Unlike every other woman I'd dated, my wife and I got along. I remember my relationships with the women before Yolanda as one long argument. I have found that women in general don't like to be outtalked. When you go out in groups, it often comes down to discussions, women on one side, men on the other. And back then, I'd be just hurling it. Often women would get quite angry. They love to be able to talk a man into submission. And with me, it never happens. They can't do it. Plus, because of the way I grew up with all my smart, talkative, opinionated siblings, I can hardly help having an argumentative nature and wouldn't if I could. I was and am a talker from a very young age. I had to be! It was a survival skill.

Yolanda puts up with that from me and even enjoys it at times—or at least finds me interesting and not boring. I feel the same about her. She and I have our disagreements, but we fundamentally like one other and like being around one another. Now it is thirty years later, and we're still going strong. I get along with her, and she gets along with me. And through all the hard times, she has been my bedrock.

Yolanda grew up in Ramseur. She was raised by her grandparents, and she had a strong attachment to her upright, hardworking grandfather. She has several sisters and brothers. Her father was quite the rolling stone. Yet she was also, in a sense, an only child—at least in her grandparents' house. She was the princess. Her sister and cousin lived nearby, but when they came to the house, she was the daughter. She stayed out with Daddy Jack and Aunt Eva, as they were called, who doted on her. Her childhood was very different from mine.

In fact, at this time, I'd better let her get a word in. After all, she's had to put up with a *lot* of my talking for over thirty years!

8

FROM YOLANDA'S SIDE

YOLANDA SPEAKS: I grew up in Ramseur, North Carolina, living with my maternal grandparents. Their last name was Brown. Mine is Hill, after my father. My mother did not marry him. Her name was Cassaundra Brown until she got married later. My mother in no way gave me up or abandoned me. We were and are as close as can be. Yet I ended up living most of my childhood with her parents.

This came about in a rather tragic way. I had a first cousin named Tanya. She was my uncle's daughter, but my grandparents were raising her as their own. One day Tanya was killed by a car. It hit her while she was outside a store when she was only seven years old.

I was two when this happened. My grandmother was devastated. She couldn't be consoled. She wanted another grandchild to stay with her for a while. We lived in Ramseur at the time, within walking distance of my grandparents. At that point, my mom was the only one of my grandmother's kids who had two children. I was two, and my sister was a baby. So I was chosen to stay with my grandmother. My mother was nearby, and I saw her constantly. It wasn't a bad transition for me at all.

Although the arrangement was supposed to be temporary, I stayed with my grandparents until I went to college. As I grew a little older, I came to love it there. My mother lived down the street. We saw each other all the time, and I would go stay at her place many times. But I had my own room at my grandparents. I *lived* there.

I began to feel that it was really my home. Plus, my grandparents spoiled me. I was the oldest grandchild, and my grandmother would often tell the other grandkids to be careful of my things at the house. I felt special. My grandmother would say to the other kids, "Don't touch that; that's Yolanda's. Put that back."

When I was eleven, my grandmother passed away from cancer. I continued to stay with my granddad at that time because, of course, I didn't want to leave him alone. So I lived there until I went to college and returned afterward. I spent weekends with my mom. By that time, my mother had moved to Greensboro. I saw her every week, and we were very close, as I said, but Daddy Jack's house was home to me.

I attended Ramseur Elementary School. At that time, it was K-8. Ramseur is a very small town. I went to high school at Eastern Randolph High School, and graduated in 1986, the same year as Mark.

* * *

My father's life is a strange tale within itself. He did not abandon me. He did not run away from my mother. He wanted to marry her. In fact, they secretly remained friends for many years. No, my father was *run off* by my grandfather in a most emphatic way.

I don't really blame my grandfather, either.

My dad's name was Alfonzo Hill. My mother was a senior in high school when she got pregnant with me. My father was two years older. He was in the Army at the time. My grandparents were very much against him marrying or having anything further to do with my mother.

Why? My dad was supersmart. He was the valedictorian of his high school, I believe. He was also an excellent athlete, well over six feet tall. He played baseball, football, and basketball. He played basketball in the military and baseball at A&T. He was extremely handsome and, obviously, a lady's man.

But that was not the problem. No, my grandparents did not like the way he grew up. They knew his relatives well, and they suspected he would be following in their footsteps. In this, they were not mistaken.

His mother, my grandmother, lived in Emporia, Virginia. When my dad was a baby, she got into a horrible accident that put her in the hospital and then in rehabilitation for years. Her son, my father, came to stay in Ramseur with my uncle and aunt, my grandmother's brother and his wife. They owned what used be called a "liquor house" in Ramseur. It wasn't legal, and that wasn't all. They also ran a small brothel attached to the house. It wasn't a full-blown den of disrepute in such a little town, but I suppose that's what it was aspiring to be. Also, the place was a gambling den.

So perhaps it wasn't surprising that my grandparents didn't want my mom to associate with the Hills of Ramseur. And, of course, my dad grew up there.

So my father didn't marry my mother, and soon he was away in the military again. I did see my dad while I was young, but he was mostly out of town. He was in Germany, and then he was in Vietnam. He was not in active combat there, but he served during the later stages of the war. When he came back from the military, he went to A&T and played baseball there.

After that, he became just what my grandparents had feared he would. You might call him a professional gambler. That was about his most respectable job. He was too smart for his own good perhaps. He'd grown up around such questionable characters and activities. Exploiting the seedy side of life seemed to come very easily to him. Fixers would fly him all around the country to gamble. He was very good at cards—and very good at cheating at cards. He sold drugs. He also ran a prostitution ring. He was, in short, a rather unsavory fellow in many respects.

Yet if you saw Alfonzo Hill, say, walking through the airport, you would think, "Oh, that's a professional man of some sort, a businessman"

He was always impeccably dressed. You would never know he was hip deep in criminal activity.

After he got out of the military, I'd see him fairly often. My mom would sneak me over because my grandparents did not want me anywhere near him. I also knew who and what he was because he had become something of a legend up in Guilford County.

His nickname was Slim Goody. That was what people called him and how they knew him.

> MARK: When I was a child, I used to get my hair cut at a place called Lowell's Barber Shop. I used to sit in the barber shop and listen to the older guys say things like, "Hey man, we went to so and so's place and guess who come by there? Slim Goody. Boy, he got a Cadillac and these girls . . ."
>
> Slim Goody was a neighborhood legend.
>
> Then doggone if I didn't grow up and marry the dread Slim Goody's daughter.

Anyway, I saw my dad at times, but my grandparents were actively against this. It was understandable, and I appreciate that. My mom and dad always remained close friends, however. He got married to someone else. Then his life took a rather bad turn.

* * *

My dad got arrested in 1978 or '79. He told me he wasn't guilty of that particular crime, and I tend to believe him. He had been saved by Christ after he was arrested but before the trial, and he had become a more truthful man as a result. Sadly, his conversion was too late to keep him from suffering the consequences of his past. Another person he used to run with broke into his home and burglarized the place, stealing a TV and other things. My father and another associate of his found out who the thief was. They went separately looking for him. The burglar's name was Lee Green.

Lee Green soon turned up murdered, shot to death. My dad said that he didn't do it, that his associate had done the killing. But because the police had been after my dad literally for years, they arrested him for the crime anyway. They knew about all his activities. They knew he had long been selling drugs, and they knew he was a middleman, transporting drugs from Florida and other states. They knew this but could never catch him in the act and prove it. They were aware of his other illegal activities as well.

The man my dad said shot Lee Green ratted out my father in order to get a reduced sentence. He told the police my dad had killed Green. At least, that's my father's story.

My dad was convicted of manslaughter. They had finally found something they could make stick to Slim Goody. His lawyer was a friend of his with whom he'd gone to high school. He is still an attorney in Greensboro. At the time, however, he was fresh out of law school and definitely not the best choice.

* * *

Dad spent the next thirty-four years in prison and got out in 2013. During my teenage years and adult life, my dad was in prison. We stayed in contact, especially after I was an adult. I went to see him often. I took our kids to see him. Mark and I went occasionally.

It may sound crazy, but my relationship with my dad was truly close. Our personalities were a lot alike, although certainly not our activities. He used to write letters to my children. The kids were close to him in their way. He had found God, was saved after accepting Christ, and was a totally changed man by that time. He was not the old Slim Goody.

We tried to get him released for a while. He was convicted on manslaughter. Someone normally doesn't spend almost forty years in prison for manslaughter, but that was the sentence under an old law. Whenever he came up for parole, his past was against him, and the parole board wouldn't set him free. He was kept in different prisons throughout North Carolina over the years. The last place he was incarcerated was a minimum-security place in Winston-Salem. I think the only reason they let him out in 2013 was because they knew he was dying of cancer. We didn't know and he didn't know, but I think the prison officials did.

Shortly after he came home, he was diagnosed with liver cancer. He died in 2015.

* * *

My grandmother Brown was a cosmetologist and also worked at a dry cleaner. My grandfather worked at a local factory in Ramseur that made yarn. It was called Ramseur Interlock. He worked there for thirty years, then retired in his fifties. After that, he went to work again. Daddy Jack was not one to let the grass grow under his feet. He went to work in Randleman for Jockey International at a factory, making socks. He ended up retiring from there around the age of sixty-five. My aunt, my mom's sister, lived practically next door. She did a lot of the cooking and cleaning after my grandmother died. It was in her house that I met Mark.

I had a great time in high school. I did well. I've always been a good student. I graduated with honors, then went to college. My great dream was to go to Oral Roberts University. I had always wanted to go to ORU and be a doctor. That was my aspiration in high school. Had my grandmother lived, I might have. We were a religious family, Baptists. My grandmother watched the evangelist Oral Roberts on TV often. But God has his way. I went to UNC Chapel Hill.

But by 1989, I had stopped going to college, and it would be years before I finished. The reason for this was perhaps unusual. A young man I had dated previously in high school turned out to be a stalker and was probably insane. I'd dated him for only a short time. I soon realized I wasn't interested, and we broke up. There wasn't any question about it. I ended it.

But after I stopped going out with him, the man began stalking me. After a year in college, my roommate Linda and I eventually got an apartment off campus. This guy—I would hardly even call him an old boyfriend—came to our apartment one day in the early evening.

He knocked at the door. My roommate and her boyfriend were also there. Almost two years after we'd dated, there he was in my apartment.

I was shocked. I had no idea what he was doing there. I took him into the kitchen to talk, and he immediately grew paranoid about my roommate and her boyfriend.

"Who is that?" he asked. "What do they want with us?"

He then picked up a knife from the counter and wielded it threateningly. That was enough. I ran from the kitchen, and we all three quickly exited the apartment, leaving him there. We sprinted to a 7-11 around the corner and called 911. He soon followed us out, jumped in his car, and cornered us at the 7-11. Fortunately, the police quickly arrived. They arrested him and took him away.

I called my mom, and she came over to Chapel Hill to pick me up. After that, I kept my eye out for this young man. I soon discovered that he was still following me. He stalked me and my best friend from high school at Randolph Mall in Asheboro. This had become a serious danger.

A few days later, I came home to my grandfather's house. I was about to open the door, and he came around the side of the house from the backyard. I started screaming. My granddaddy heard me crying out and opened the door.

And this man tried to fight my granddaddy.

He *bit* my granddaddy's hand. My grandfather had to have stitches in his finger.

But my grandaddy was not a weak man. He managed to push the stalker away and told the guy off in no uncertain terms. He said we'd better not ever see him around there again. My mother called the guy's mother—his family lived in Ramseur—and said, "Listen, your son is going to get killed if he goes around there again."

The young man ended up dying about ten years later, I believe from complications of sickle cell anemia. I hope he got the help he so desperately needed before that.

All of this frightened me a great deal—so much so that I decided to take some time off from college and move back home. That's why I wasn't in school and was at my aunt's house when I met Mark in March of 1989.

Mark may have considered himself a dissipated wretch at the time, but this was far from the truth in my eyes. He was gentlemanly and protective. He was kind and forbearing. After my harrowing experience with the stalker, he truly seemed a knight in shining armor.

I still lived next door with my grandfather, but I spent a lot of time at my aunt's house in Ramseur. I had cousins who were around my age. That was why I was at my aunt's house, sitting at her kitchen bar area when Mark walked in. My cousin Robert, who was two years younger than I, was dating Mark's friend Anthony's sister, Lynn Spearman.

MARK: We were going to drop Lynn off and go on, but she said, "Naw, y'all got to come in and meet everybody." She made us come in.

Meeting Mark wasn't a lightning strike at first. We said hello. He and his friend left, and Lynn stayed. That evening, Lynn talked Mark up to me quite a bit.

"That guy Mark, don't you think he's cute? Y'all should go out."

I wasn't too enthusiastic.

She said, "No, I'm going to set it up."

I said, "Okay, Lynn, if you say so."

She's a sweetheart. And that's what she did. Mark and I went on our first date.

MARK: Somebody told me to be there, and I showed up. I have no doubt it was Lynn.

Yes, Lynn did it. She set up our first date. She's a matchmaker. We even met at her house before we went out. We went to the movies at James Theater in Greensboro. It's not there anymore. We saw *Bill and Ted's Excellent Adventure*. Stupidest movie ever.

MARK: Are you kidding? It is a great movie. So-crates! Come on, So-crates!

I remember very little about the movie. We sat and talked in the lobby afterward. I realized at that point that Mark talked—a lot. I was reserved at the time. It was almost overwhelming.

After that first date, I spoke to Lynn and agreed that Mark was nice. We ended up going out again. Well, we dated for a month or so, and he grew on me. He was super-handsome. We were younger and thinner back then. He's been in the military and the reserves. He was still muscular and had his cowboy boots on all the time. Cute.

And he talked. And talked. He loved movies, so he talked about movies. He was interested in all the genres of music. He was extremely nice and polite and always respectful, a gentleman. He opened doors for me, all that good stuff. I remember speaking to my aunt Dana about him. By then, Mark had been to some of my family get-togethers, and she had met him. I was standing in her bedroom doorway one day, discussing things, and she said, "How's your man? He's very nice."

"Yeah, but he talks too much," I said. "I'm not really that into him because of that."

Aunt Dana shook her head. "Don't you give up on him because he's a good guy. He talks too much? If that's the only thing that's wrong with him, that's not bad."

So I didn't give up on Mark for talking.

However, I was not the only one who noticed. My mom had moved to Greensboro when I was around ten. I was at my mom's house, and he'd come over. We were in the living room discussing this and that. When he left, my mom, who had been listening, came out and told me, "You know, that's a nice guy, but he sure doesn't ever shut up."

She actually liked Mark a lot. My mom worked for a company called Blue Bell, whom ended up becoming Wrangler. One of her best friends was Gloria Bynum, who she had met at work. It turned out that Mark's dad, Dayson, and Gloria's father, Pinese, were brothers. Gloria and Mark were first cousins. Gloria and my mother were close, and I had grown up around Gloria's children. So there was that connection.

After our first date, we were—not officially yet—a couple. We never broke up or dated anyone else after that. We met in February of 1989 and got married in May of 1990. We either talked every day or saw each other. This was before cell phones were common, so we spent a lot of time on the house phones.

He asked me to marry him on the phone. He was on a work trip for Sbarro in Virginia, helping open a store there. I think that was the first time since we'd met that we had been apart for a long period of time.

By that time, I'd realized that Mark wasn't *just* yammering. He was extremely intelligent, super-smart. That is what I've always found most attractive about him over the years. Back then, he talked about things that most people at twenty simply weren't talking about, weren't equipped to talk about. I was impressed with his intelligence and never got bored.

I was on my grandfather's phone when Mark asked me to marry him. By this time, I was just visiting Daddy Jack's. I had been living with my mother in Greensboro for a time, then Mark and I had moved in together. Mark had an apartment after he started working at Sbarro, and I was ready to get my own place again. So we lived together.

That apartment cost around $400 a month, and, boy, we thought that was a lot of money. Moving in together seemed more momentous at the time than getting married. The apartment was in Greensboro, the Yorktown Apartments. My granddaddy liked Mark, but he did not approve of this arrangement—at all.

MARK: Neither did my mama.

Our living out of wedlock wasn't very popular with our parents.

MARK: That's probably what played into my asking her to marry me. We both grew up in church.

We knew it was wrong to just live together.

MARK: Yes, we knew we shouldn't do that. So the marriage was more like, "We need to fix this."

83

At that point we were still going to our separate churches.

> MARK: I had joined her church, but I was going back and forth between there and St. Stephen.

We got married in my church, Oakland Baptist Church, in Ramseur. Sundays were a big deal. My whole family went to that church. After church on Sundays, we'd all get together and have dinner or grill and play badminton in the backyard. It was family time. I think Mark liked that my family was so close and tight. We celebrated every birthday, every accomplishment. His family didn't do that as much. My whole family embraced him as part of our family.

Our son Dayson was born when we were living in the apartment, in July of 1990. You can put the numbers together. We were married in May of 1990. This was another reason for getting married. Dayson was a beautiful baby, nine pounds, two ounces. I went through nineteen hours of hard labor at Moses Koane Hospital. My mom and my aunt and Mark were in the room with me when he arrived.

By the time I had our daughter Kim, we had rented a house. I took a job at United Guarantee Mortgage Insurance. We moved to Ramseur for a few months of 1992 after that. Mark went to work at Klaussner not long after Kim was born. We moved back to Greensboro in 1993, where I worked at Aetna Insurance. Mark drove back and forth from Asheboro to Klaussner.

Then I opened the daycare in 2000. We had preschoolers and after-schoolers, from zero to twelve. Mark worked a lot with the after-schoolers.

* * *

Mark and I were a unit. We have been from the start. I could not have written a prototype that was better for "best dad." He's very creative, kind of artsy. He played so many games with the children. He was and is a hands-on dad. He changed diapers. It's always been a team effort.

This has translated to Mark's political life. We are still a team.

In 1996, we bought our first house. Kim was four, and Dayson was six. That was the house they grew up in. Families were everywhere on our cul-de-sac. We tried to give them the quintessential childhood.

MARK: But we failed in some ways. That's the house that we lost, that was repossessed. After that, it seemed like we got shoved into the wilderness. We had been wasting money and time. I wasted a lot of time. We learned more during the period after we lost the house than when we were in the house. We had a better time in the house. But we learned more after.

Yes.

Our son Dayson is still single. He works for me at my business. Our daughter Kim is an assistant district attorney in Guilford County. She's married and has our two grandbabies.

9

GETTING SERIOUS

DUE TO Lynn Spearman's machinations, Yolanda and I eventually went out on our first date. Yes, we saw that masterpiece *Bill and Ted's Excellent Adventure*, a memory we laugh about to this day. I realized that she was a woman who was very easy to talk to. She says I talk a lot, but Yolanda could carry a conversation about almost anything. Yolanda was unlike any woman I had ever met. She liked what she liked and did not mind saying what she felt needed to be said. Yolanda was not concerned with fitting into a mold. I was at ease with her, and she fascinated me. There was a part of me that was just waiting for the time when I would say or do something stupid to mess it all up, but that never happened. When we began seeing each other, I was still going off to complete my reserve drills. By the time I fulfilled my commitment to the Army reserves, we were seriously dating. This was when I decided to become part of the individual ready reserves.

At this time, Yolanda and I made a huge mistake and fell into a deep sin. I spoke about this years ago in a Facebook post. Recently the post has resurfaced, and I addressed it again. Here are the facts: before we were married and before we had kids, Yolanda and I had an abortion. It was the hardest decision we have ever made. Sadly, we made the wrong one. This decision has been with us ever since. It's because of this experience, and our spiritual journey, that we are so adamantly pro-life today. We know what it's like to be in that situation. We know the pain that an abortion causes.

For everyone who has had that experience and carries that burden, we want you to know you are not alone. Furthermore, we have a Savior who forgives us of our sins and offers us grace. No one is perfect. No one is too far gone to be saved. The pain that this experience has caused Yolanda and me is one of the reasons we are so pro-life.

In May of 1990, Yolanda and I were married. We were soon blessed with a son, Dayson Hugh. My perspective on life changed immediately upon the birth of my son. I saw before me, in his little face, a responsibility. I was the one God had given charge over this child. I had to be a responsible man. When Dayson was born, I was working as an assistant manager at a Sbarro's pizza restaurant at Four Seasons Mall in Greensboro. While going to work there each day, I would think, "This is not it; this cannot be it. Seven dollars an hour is not going to cut it with a family." I knew I had to seriously consider working toward a career, not just holding down any job.

I was blessed at this time to have family members and friends who could help me in my search for work. My wife's uncle was instrumental. He was a long-time employee of a local furniture plant in the area. He helped me to get on at that plant. That is where I learned to upholster furniture.

My position at Klaussner Manufacturing was the first "real job" I ever had. Klaussner was the first place I made enough money to support a family. There I made a wage far above the minimum wage. I thought I had arrived. My wife and I looked at a house at a place called Wooley Ridge. It was a big, two-story house on a hill. It seemed like a dream house to us. We asked the agent, "How much does this house cost?" She said it was $115,000.

Woah. We said thank you and left. But we got to thinking: I could use my GI bill benefits, and my earnings would probably qualify us for a loan. We could get this house. And so we did.

At Klaussner Furniture, I was an upholsterer. I started at the entry level and built what they call "panels." These are wooden sections of good furniture. Every technique you need in upholstery you can learn from understanding how to build a panel, from how to cleat something, to how to welt something, and how to cut something to make it fit. I learned how to make stripes line up. That's why they start out all inexperienced people building panels. You can do almost anything else after you master the skill.

You start out on an upholstery line, doing what's called "outside." Outside is putting on arms, closing up the backs, putting on black-bottom—basically finishing the piece. The further you go down the line to the beginning, the more experienced the people are. For instance, the person who puts in the seat deck is the most experienced hand. That seat deck is going to determine how everything else on the chair lines up. The deck has to be put in just right. The next most experienced people are going to be the "back men." They put the back in, which determines how well the arms go in. They've got to line up the back with the seat. Next are the arm people. They have to be experienced because a lot of time they're going to be putting pleats in the upholstery fabric. Then the last stage is the outside people.

Everything was done at workstations. At Klaussner, each person had what's called a bunk, a place to put the piece you are working on. The seat guy puts the seat in and passes it to the back man. That person passes it on to the arm man, and then to the outside, and the outside passes it on down to the inspector. That's how they roll with it. The place was divided into lines, or styles, of furniture pieces, and each line got progressively more difficult until you got down to the leather and rich fabric furniture, although there was no leather man in our particular factory. That was where the most experienced guys worked, the ones who made the most money.

Line Five was the line everybody wanted to be on because all those guys were making $200 to $300 per day. They were going home at one o'clock and were all guys who had been there thirty years or so. And that's where we all aspired to be. We wanted to work on Line Five or be a "floater," filling in anywhere and everywhere. Floaters, too, were better paid.

Upholstering is like a football team. You have people who are great at it. You have people who are just okay. You have people in the middle. I was one of the guys in the middle. I wasn't great at it. I wasn't terrible at it. I was a good worker, however.

Unfortunately, I came into Klaussner at a time they were about to make a major change because of what was going on with NAFTA. When I got there, Sears, Montgomery Ward, Heilig-Meyers, and places like them were buying a ton of furniture from us. They were selling it on the cheap with what are sometimes called "easy credit rip-offs." They would rent you furniture and then repossess it if you didn't keep up payments. We were selling to many Rent-A-Centers and establishments like that. The good times were seemingly rolling, but trouble was ahead.

At places like Heilig-Meyers, the credit crunch started to hit. The money began to come due, and they didn't have it. Sears and Montgomery Ward went out of business for all intents and purposes. Both are gone now. And then NAFTA crashed in, and other places started disappearing. The work began to go to China. So my time was reduced, and reduced again. I ended up leaving because I just couldn't get the hours I needed to earn a living wage. It was a slow-motion layoff.

But in the early '90s, I was earning a good salary. I was making $125 to $150 per day on production. Our daughter, Kimberly Evana, was born, and Yolanda and I were enjoying life. Every year, during the week of July 4, the furniture plant would close. We would take the family to the beach for a vacation that week. The plant would also close the week of Christmas, so I had a second week of built-in vacation time. We would have a great Christmas with piles of presents under the tree. We were also able to move into our new house. My wife was working,

I was working, life was good, our finances seemed stable, and we were happy. At that point in my life I thought, "I have arrived. I'm going to work in furniture, live in this big house on a hill, and raise our kids." But there was disaster lying in wait.

In the mid-'90s, things began to change. The North American Free Trade Agreement (NAFTA) had gone into effect. Jobs at the plant began to dry up, and the company was losing money. At this time, I was not as politically aware as I am now. Yet I was becoming more interested in what was going on in our nation. I did not understand, however, why our successful furniture plant was losing money and jobs. One of my supervisors explained to me that NAFTA was the ultimate reason. He predicted that in time it would put all plants like ours out of business. This particular supervisor was always cursing politicians and the government, which in turn made me more interested in the political landscape. Sure enough, due to the implications of NAFTA, I eventually had to leave my job. My salary had been cut so much that I could no longer afford to work there. I had to start all over again, and it nearly ruined us financially.

I didn't lose my job at Klaussner; I quit because I wasn't making enough money because they didn't have enough work. I was going in at seven in the morning, getting off at ten o'clock a.m. and making fifty dollars a day—maybe. I was hardly working. I wasn't earning enough to pay our bills by any stretch of the imagination.

The combination of NAFTA and, to be honest, bad choices when it came to money, put us in a financial trap we couldn't escape. I was guilty of bad money management; when I had money and should have been putting it in the bank or spending it on essential things, such as getting ahead on house payments, I was just throwing money away. For example, we were going to the beach every summer, spending a lot of money to stay right at the shore when we could have stayed inland for much less and still spent just as much time at the beach. It was foolishness, absolute foolishness. And it was then that I got upside down on our house mortgage

It took years, but we finally lost the house to foreclosure. I'm well aware that this was the same thing that happened to my mom. It was a hard lesson to learn, a very tough lesson. My wife and I spent some difficult years after we lost that home. We had to recover. We learned a lot of hard facts about how to spend money and how not to spend money. If we had made some different personal decisions earlier, the outcome might have been better. Maybe not better *enough,* though. A rolling economic disaster was hitting the workers of middle America. Jobs were being shipped overseas in the name of efficiency—but actually as a result of bad deals that punished American workers through government mandates. It was after I left the job at Klaussner—only a part-time non-job by then—that we really started getting behind.

When I left the job at Klaussner, I had to start over again at Papa John's, starting in the basement at eight bucks an hour and having to work my way up. I did end up a general manager. But in meantime, we got further and further behind on the house.

Klaussner Furniture survived NAFTA. It's still there, in a lesser form. The immediate problem proved to be the improvident Rent-A-Center deals the company was making, but NAFTA played a role in damaging the company as well. Furniture making was huge in North Carolina, in the town of High Point in particular. NAFTA decimated that city. For a time, the city of High Point looked like a ghost town due to the economic destruction. Now things are coming back, but there is still a long way to go—and the possibility looms that it may never recover if ignorant government policies continue, or even worse ones from the past are reinstated.

10

THE RAILROAD IS DAHNGEROUS!

THANKFULLY, I knew how to do restaurant work, and I had a friend working at a local pizza restaurant, a Papa John's franchise. I was able to get a part-time job with him, working the second shift. I did not want to work in the restaurant business again. But I saw there was an opportunity for growth, and I was never afraid to put in the effort when called on. Eventually I worked my way up to the position of general manager of the restaurant. I was finally earning good money again, but this took time. It took time to climb that ladder, and the job took time away from my family. My children were in school, and I was missing out on many events in their lives. I knew I ought to rethink my career once again. Eventually I left. I also decided I should go back to school and pursue the education I had not been ready for as a teenager.

I secured a job at an aviation services company and enrolled once again at NC A&T. I began taking classes, again with hopes of finishing with a communications major. Then, while I was working and going to school, my wife decided to open an in-home daycare center. By God's grace, it became extremely successful. Soon she was no longer able to operate the business out of our home and moved to a freestanding building.

Eventually, Yolanda suggested that I work with her full-time. I decided to leave the aviation company and stopped my college classes. We worked together at the daycare for about seven years, from 2000 to 2007.

The daycare was in a lower middle-class neighborhood. Some parents were private pay, while others were paid for by the county. The socioeconomic status of the families was mixed and didn't apply to any race in a stereotypical way. It was a wonderful mix of children and parents of all backgrounds. We had parents who were firemen and factory workers, and parents who were teachers, all kinds. It was in Greensboro on Rambling Road. It's still there, though we don't own it anymore.

I had a fantastic experience there. Working with those children was one of the most rewarding experiences in my life. They found a special place in our hearts. I saw potential in so many of them. For example, one little boy was the funniest and most athletic child I had ever seen. I told my wife, "One day that child is going to play football." Sure enough, today he is playing football at a college in Georgia. We keep in contact with many of the kids from our daycare and keep abreast of what they are doing in life. Most of them are young adults and in college now.

Working with those children gave me more insight into my passions and talents as well. As I interacted with and exposed them to a variety of historical and cultural events and activities, I realized how much I loved history and enjoyed teaching it to the children at daycare. For example, one time I decided to challenge them to learn the preamble to the United States Constitution. I promised twenty dollars to the first kid who could recite it to me without any mistakes. Those kids worked quite hard, and a boy named Jesse was the first to successfully recite the preamble. It was during this time that I decided I would love to teach history. I knew I wanted to return to college, but this time I planned to get a degree in history. I had ambitions to keep going until I could teach at the college level.

WE ARE THE MAJORITY!

I loved working at our daycare center. There were moments of pure joy. I remember when I was in the little amphitheater at a local mall. I was surrounded by a bunch of kids, eating ice cream. I thought, "I'm at the mall eating ice cream with kids and having fun, going to the movies in the middle of a summer day, sitting at the movies watching some kids' movie on Imax—this is not work."

The days we went to the children's museum or were outside in the backyard of the center playing a game of football or some other sport gave me joy. Or being inside the daycare center on what we called Fun Fridays playing with Thomas the Tank Engine. I used to do all kinds of crazy voices for the trains. I would put the tracks down, and we'd run the trains. I had one voice, a sort of a French accent and I would say, "Be *vewy* careful, the railroad makes many *dahngers*. It is *dahngerous!*"

And all the kids would tell their parents when they came to pick them up, "The railroad is dahngerous!"

My wife recently ran into one of our former charges working at Dario's in Kernersville while he goes to college. He was so tiny then. He's a great big man now. Another one works for a prosecutor's office in Maryland. It's crazy. I encounter a lot of them on social media. They grew up and are doing amazing things.

Working in daycare is what solidified my desire to be a teacher. I had two reasons. One, I love history. The second is that in every job I've worked, in some capacity in some way, I was picked to be either a leader or a teacher.

* * *

Financial hardships, losing or changing jobs, and crazy hours can often put a strain on marriages. I can say that through all the ups and downs we had experienced in the workforce; Yolanda and I have never felt that particular strain. We were a team with a common goal. We had a common faith in God, and we loved our children. We knew it was our responsibility to work, provide, and care for our family. I may have made some bad decisions in life, but being with Yolanda more than balances all of them.

The daycare always had clients. But that is a tough business to keep afloat. People would come in our doors, and so many of them would think we were making hundreds of thousands of dollars and were rich. I wanted to say, "You *do* realize we're living just about like you are, paycheck to paycheck." We had clients. The business was running well. We had all the things that we needed. We paid our bills. "But it ain't easy," I wanted to say to them. "We're not making a fortune by any means."

Now, for me, the most stressful thing I did all day was mop the floor and help keep things clean at the daycare. But for Yolanda, who had the primary responsibility of operating the business, stress levels were high. Not only did she have the responsibility of caring for children, but she had to deal with things, such as parents who wouldn't pay when they should and other complications. Over and above that, while working at the daycare, I saw firsthand how the government can overburden small businesses. It was hard at times to operate effectively because there were so many regulations and red tape.

The paperwork was unremitting and seemed to increase every year. Eventually Yolanda had had enough. She got another job, and the management began falling on me more. That's when we decided to sell the daycare. By the time we sold the business, our personal finances were not good, either. We got what we could for the daycare, paying off what we could.

Looking back, working at the daycare helped me to see the difficult implications of government involvement in small business. That was one of the main reasons my wife decided to sell the business. She no longer wanted to deal with the frustrations of running the daycare under so much red tape.

The daycare is still in operation today. After selling it in 2007, Yolanda worked at American Express for several years. In 2011, she decided to return to college at UNCG. There she finished up her undergraduate courses and went on to earn her master's degree in 2015.

Before selling the daycare, we had lost our house to foreclosure. It was devastating. We had to move into an apartment. The kids had to change schools. It was bad.

I call this our "time in the wilderness."

11

THE WILDERNESS

WE MOVED three times during this period, first to an apartment, then to a town house, and finally to a rented house. It was a hard time for my kids. They were in elementary and middle school and had to transfer to different schools. My son ended up at Allen Middle School, my daughter at Guilford Middle School, and they both went to Grimsley High School, just as I had, but my daughter eventually graduated from another Greensboro high school.

Kids go along. They are resilient to a degree. We spent a number of years rebuilding our lives, trying to do it right. My kids laugh about it now, but we all remember well that there was a summer in the town house when we had no hot water because I couldn't afford the gas bill. It was rough.

Then we moved to our rental house on Sassafras Court. We stayed there for quite a while. I used to sit in that little house and think, "When are we ever going to get out of here?" We dreamed of owning another house. Yolanda used to watch HGTV and imagine our next home. To me, it seemed so far away, like it was never going to happen.

By 2011, Yolanda went back to school, eventually completing a master's degree—and I went back into furniture manufacturing. I got a job working part-time on second shift with a company in High Point. I worked my way up and was blessed to become a zone leader. A zone leader was a supervisory position. While working there, I was making enough money to sustain our household with my children and my wife attending college full-time.

* * *

All was not doom and gloom, by any means. We were never that sort of family. As for me, I rediscovered—or rather reawakened—my almost obsessive youthful love of trains, but this time in a far less self-destructive and semi-insane manner, working with the kind of trains that probably can't kill you.

I got into model railroading.

This was a reawakened passion, actually. I had begun to truly learn about trains, the trivia and details, after I got married and was working at Sbarro at the mall. For the first time, I had a tiny bit of disposable income. When I was a kid, I did have model railroad sets. I would put the track down and run the train around. I didn't know how to wire a layout. I just put track all over the floor and ran it the best I could.

The first time I ever did a real layout was when we were living in the apartment. I got a board and laid the track. I nailed it down and put in switches and wiring. I bought engines and painted them. I began to encounter the details, the lore, of trains.

I learned what a tuxedo scheme was. I learned the sizes and types of the boxcars: fifty-foot, forty-foot, reefers, gondolas, center-flow hoppers. There was a train shop in downtown Greensboro called Big John's Little Trains. It was by the crossing where Blumenthal's department store had once been, the perfect spot for a train shop. I rode the bus to work, so while I was waiting, I would go into Big John's and look at my favorite brand, Anthearn. The Anthearn trains and equipment came in containers called the Anthearn Blue Box because the boxes were blue.

You could buy anything and everything to equip your layout.

I am currently in the midst of completing a grand layout at my home office. When I finish the layout, my train engines will be made by Anthearn. These days, the wonderful world of digital switching has arrived.

Back when I first started with model railroads, it was all direct current, DC. You had to wire up your layout in analog fashion. If you wanted to run more than one train, you had to make up blocks of transformers and complete lots of other complicated wiring.

That first layout in my tiny apartment was great. I had several custom-painted engines. I learned how to do weathering to make them realistic.

I did no more model railroading for a long time after that—for fifteen years or more. I did not go back until we lost the first house and moved into our town house. It was there that I discovered something called eBay.

At that time, people were selling junk on eBay. And a lot of the junk they were selling was old trains from their attics and basements. I would get super-cheap Anthearn engines that back in the day, brand new, would have cost twenty dollars or more. Now I bought them on eBay for two bucks. I was able to build quite a layout for next to nothing. I think I might have spent in total three hundred bucks putting together that particular layout. I was buying boxcars on eBay for a dollar fifty. Some boxcars with no wheels I got even cheaper, and I'd pick up a bag of wheels from somebody for two dollars.

I built a model railroad layout, a very nice model railroad layout, on a shoestring budget. That was the first time I built an honest-to-God layout with scenery. People would come by, and the first thing they would do is head back to the sunroom and look at that model railroad. It was the coolest thing in the house.

I learned about how the real railroad operates from model railroading. It is a very hands-on way to study history and economics. I highly recommend it.

* * *

Where I'm at now with model railroading is what they call realistic operations. I'm truly learning how the railroad works. I have friends who work for the railroad, who have told me how a yard operates and how sidings work, and that's what I'm incorporating into my current layout. I want mine to operate like a real railroad. If it doesn't make sense, I don't want it on there. I'm not like the guys who build a railroad and have aliens land on it. That's fine. That's their vision. But my vision is to build a model railroad that represents the Greensboro railroad that I remember from 1975 to 1980.

Yolanda says she doesn't like my hobby. But she loves it. She likes to tell people about it. She thinks it's strange, and it is. My relationship with the railroad is bizarre. I admit it. I ride down the streets and see a train—I'm enraptured. I call trains "big dirties," because they are. They're big, dirty pieces of equipment. So I'll see them, and I'll say, "There he is right there. There's a big dirty, and he's trying to hide from me, but I see him." It's like your best friend who you're always calling Ugly Dope, but you know you love him. That's my relationship with trains.

The train layout itself is very organized. But my tools are everywhere, and it's making me itch right now, just thinking about it. No more DC. Now we have DCC, digital command and control. There's a controller that sends a unique signal to each train, and each train has its own decoder in it. You program your train to the box. You put a number on it. When you select one number, the train goes one direction. Put in another, it goes the opposite. So Train One and Train Two can go clockwise, counterclockwise, or however you want. You can have five trains running in five different directions. You don't have to block off everything like the old days, either. DCC is the best thing to happen to model trains. I'll never go back.

Before I leave this earth, what one thing do I want more than anything? My own tiny railroad on my own property. Doggone, I'm going to get it! Live steam is what they call those miniature trains you can ride on. You can get a locomotive for about thirty-five grand. What really costs money is the tracks and ties—a couple hundred thousand at least.

It's a dream. Maybe one day. Maybe it doesn't have to be *my* property. For example, it might be a lawn in Raleigh owned by the people of North Carolina and used with their permission. Of course I'd give all the citizens free rides! It might be one in Washington, DC. That would be pretty cool. Everybody would be standing there saying, "Look at that dern fool having fun. Can I ride?"

You bet. All aboard!

* * *

A little while before we sold the daycare center, I went to a temporary agency to find a job. They sent me to Thomasbilt Buses. It was not a good place to work. One night they pulled a bunch of us into the break room and told us "We got to let y'all go because the union is mad because we have too many temps in the building." I was very happy to hear that. I couldn't stand that place.

I left there, and the temp agency sent me over to a manufacturer called Steelcase. I walked through the door and realized I could be comfortable there. I knew how to upholster. I could make a real job out of it. I started part-time on second shift and did that for a number of weeks. I was good at it.

Their brand of upholstering was nothing like Klaussner. Klaussner was what I call "real" upholstery. That's where you had a piece of cloth, and you took that piece of cloth, cut it, and fit it to the back. Or if you had an arm, you laid the cloth onto that arm and crafted it onto that foam arm and put the pleats in it.

Steelcase was sock-on furniture. The back was sewed by a bunch of sewers, and you gathered it up under the furniture and made sure it was all tucked in nice and neat. But because of my training at Klaussner, I was very fast and also very skilled doing it. I moved up from second shift part-time to first shift full-time, and eventually became a regular employee. I stayed doing only upholstery for a number of years, and then decided to step up and become what's called a zone leader. I took and passed the classes, got promoted, and held that position for my last five years at Steelcase.

Steelcase was run with what's called a lean manufacturing process. In this system, you have zones, each having a different sort of work. You have frame building and glue up. You have cut. You have sewing. You have upholstery. Each zone has a zone leader. I was an upholstery line zone leader. It's not a supervisory system. They got rid of most of the supervisors and kept only three for the entire building. Everything else was run by zone leaders. It's almost like running your own little shop inside the business. Basically, you do something of everything.

I had a fantastic experience at Steelcase. There were some difficult days, but I had more good days than bad days there. I learned a whole lot, especially about managing and working with people. I get super-excited when I start talking about lean manufacturing, which is what was used there.

Hey, I still believe that if you don't run your business by lean manufacturing, there's something wrong with you. That is a great way to run a business. But it's got to be done right. Lean manufacturing makes things safer and smoother. You don't work nearly as hard. It takes discipline to do it, however. I've been drawing on that ever since. I use the method in everything I do in both life and work.

An example: at Steelcase, we had a giant order for a style of chair called Catherine chairs. We probably had to build four or five thousand. We needed to hire a bunch of temps to help us. We didn't have enough people.

My old boss-man picked me to set up a line full of temps. Not one of the people on that line had ever upholstered *anything*. They'd never operated a staple gun. Some of them probably couldn't wrap Christmas presents. He gave me the task of teaching them how to upholster a very high-end chair.

I thought, *This man is crazy.* But I taught them how to upholster those chairs from the frame up, and before long, we were right next to what was called the Catherine Line, people who had been building Catherine chairs for years. And we were outpacing those people two-to-one.

I taught my team through lean manufacturing standards.

"When you finish cutting here, you take your scissors and put them exactly in this place." This would position them for the next cut.

"When you finished doing this, you set the glue gun right here."

They learned by that standard, which was the one I was using. And I was known for working fast and efficiently by using those lean standards. People I worked with for years couldn't understand how I could build a chair so fast. It was simply by using the lean manufacturing techniques.

When I was building a Catherine chair, I had a pad on which I had sketched out where to lay my tools between tasks. When I got done with a tool, it went right back to the same place on the pad. When I was finished with scissors, they went here. The staple gun went to its particular place. When I finished with the glue gun, it went to its own slot. When I cut, I grabbed the scrap pieces and threw them in the waste can. When I was done for the day, I didn't have leather all over the floor to sweep up. I didn't have tools scattered all over my desk and didn't need to search for my scissors. My scissors were right there, within the lines.

Every so often, I would rethink the positioning. I would consider my scissors, for instance. They are sitting there, but I'm going to pick them up and move to the cutting position—why not set them down directly under the next cutting position? Those are the sorts of changes I made. And that is the discipline part. When you get ready to set those scissors down, you have to get in the habit of putting them in the new, better place or turn them the new way. You have to erase the old mark, redraw the new one, and stick to your decision until it becomes a habit.

That was part of the magic that explains how I could build things faster than most everyone there. They would finish a chair piece, and I'd be waiting for them to give me the next one. That's also how I taught the new people to work. Soon they were outpacing guys that had been there ten to fifteen years.

Some people call that control of your movements robotic, or even lazy. I call it smart. Another example. Everybody had dustpans. At the end of the shift, everyone was bent over sweeping into their dustpans. I liked my back too much for that. I decided to make a dustpan like the guy at the mall. You know the one I mean, with the long handle and the flip-down pan.

I put a dustpan on a stick at first, but that didn't work. So I went to Lowe's Hardware one day and bought a premade stand-up dustpan. I brought it in and began to use it. Another zone leader saw me. I swept some trimmings up and dumped them, then she said, "Oh my God, how lazy!"

And I thought, "Really? Because I'm not bending over sweeping dust in my face? That's not lazy."

I just smiled and shook my head.

A couple of days later I went to get my dustpan off my rack, but it wasn't there. I looked around. Who had it? That zone leader. Before long everybody in the whole place had them.

As an example of how *not* to do it, right now something's driving me crazy! I'm working on the model railroad at home, and I have junk everywhere. Every time I go up there, I want to take all that stuff and throw it in the trash. I want to set that room on fire because it's such a mess. Traditionally, I keep things like that so *organized*. But lately I'm having to rush around so much that I don't have time to keep things the way I like them, and it's really driving me nuts!

* * *

At Steelcase, I was an upholsterer and a zone leader. I learned a lot while working at this company. I realized much about myself, made many new friends, and enjoyed being an integral part of making the business successful.

During this time I also returned to college, but instead I enrolled at Guilford Technical Community College to finish the general education classes I still needed. After completing those classes. I transferred to the University of North Carolina at Greensboro (UNCG). This time, I did not decide to reenroll without a plan. I was working my way to a degree in history for the purpose of becoming a teacher. I had direction. I had a purpose in mind. I knew I had to use the resources the school provided to help me achieve my goal. This effort was totally different for me as I worked and took classes. Everything was going well and seemed stable, but there were strains.

My wife was in graduate school. My daughter was in high school. My son was in college. I was the only person in the house working. We were struggling financially. I was paying the bills, but barely. The lady who owned the house we rented—her name was Mary Hall—was good to us. If she had been a real stickler, we'd have been out. There were times I got two or three months behind on rent, and she would say, "Just give me something." I'd give her fifty bucks, and she'd let it slide for an extra month. Our rent would get caught up, then we'd get behind for a while, then we'd pay it back. It was a cycle that was hard to escape.

Steelcase in High Point, North Carolina, was started by a man named Paul Braden. The company was called Braden International at first. Steelcase bought out Braden, and "Braden International" was still on the sign when I first went to work there. The furniture we built in that factory was called the Coalesse brand. For a mill-grade, four-seat sofa with leather, you were talking $15,000. It was high-end office furniture.

Yet I saw the handwriting on the wall. After experiencing what NAFTA did to Klaussner, I knew they wouldn't survive if the country's political economics did not change. I knew they would shut the doors eventually. For a long time, all management ever talked about was "globalism, globalism."

"We're a global company."

And I was like, "Yeah, you're going to take this global company to Mexico."

And indeed NAFTA reared its head again. The zone leaders in our facility received a message to bring all our employees to the main office. At that meeting, we were told the company would shut down our plant and move the factory to Mexico.

Mexico!

WE ARE THE MAJORITY!

That's what they did. They shut down the plant in High Point and moved the entire operation to Mexico. It was a gradual thing. Not only did they move the plant to Mexico, but they brought workers from Mexico to our plant and *had us train them*. Talk about a slap in the face! The Mexican workers generally did great. But there was this guy and girl they brought up once, and the two of them just vanished. A free ride to the good, old US!

The day they began to shut the place down was very sad. I was sad, but mostly for the workers who were stuck in the middle. They hadn't been there long enough to retire with full benefits, but you knew they were probably too old to start something completely new.

I watched over the next year and a half as 350 people lost their jobs at Steelcase. It was a very difficult time for many of them. Some had dedicated decades to this company and planned to retire from there, but the proverbial carpet was pulled out from under their feet. In some ways, it was the best of times. I saw how honorably those affected handled what had happened. On the other hand, it was the worst of times, for it was extremely sad to see so many lose their jobs. Some think NAFTA was a good thing overall because the positives, they say, outweigh the negatives. In other words, the list of "pros" was longer than the "cons." However, I saw how NAFTA and federal policy destroyed many people's livelihoods. The hard truth came right to my doorstep not once, but twice. I have never considered NAFTA a good thing. Not then, and not now.

It took some time for operations to cease completely at our plant. I left a few months before the final shutdown.

To Steelcase's credit, they did what they could to take care of those folks. And I believe they have regretted shutting that plant down ever since. The winds of change sometimes blow in the other direction too.

* * *

I got a lump sum of money when Steelcase fled to Mexico. I thought I was going to get money from the federal government as well to go back to school, but that turned out to be a pipe dream.

I believed what I was going to do was go to school, because that's what they assured me I could do. They told me, "We'll pay you while you're in school." But when I went to the unemployment office, I was disappointed.

The worker there asked me, "What are you going to study in school?"

I said, "history."

"For what? How is that *retraining*?"

"I want to retrain as a history professor, a teacher," I replied.

And they replied, "There's not any payment program here for history. You sure you don't want to be an electrician or something similar? We're talking about lateral motion. That's not going to fit the criteria."

And I told them I wasn't going to change my mind because that is what I wanted to do.

I didn't receive any aid. I went to school while I was collecting unemployment, and when that ran out in 2015, I knew I had to get to work. I went to a temp agency and got placed working for twelve dollars an hour at a furniture frame-building shop. I continued searching diligently for something permanent.

Finally, I applied at a place called Davis Furniture.

No job available.

Too bad. I had really liked the looks of the place.

Then I realized I'd forgotten something, a notebook I'd left at the interview. Yet I had to go to work.

I worked that day, then returned to get my notebook. When I did, Jeff Manuel, an HR guy at Davis, came out and asked, "Hey, are you still looking for a job?"

I said, "Yeah, I certainly am." Then he said, "Well, come back tomorrow and we'll make you an offer."

I did just that. The next day, I got handed a written offer in an envelope. I opened it up in the car, and I remember how excited I was. I called my wife and said, "These guys are going to pay me eighteen dollars an hour!"

We were very happy. That's why I still feel attached to Davis Furniture to this day and love those people to death. I worked overtime, sixty hours a week. I got my rent caught up in short order.

I'd get my paycheck on Wednesday, go to the bank and cash it, and head straight over to Mary Hall's house to pay our rent. And I did that until I got the rent caught up as well.

We stayed caught up thereafter. And during that time, something else wonderful happened.

My wife finished school and started the nonprofit organization she runs now. It's called Balanced Nutrition. She's the administrator and works with daycare centers that feed their low-income children, using federal and state money to pay for food. They get reimbursed per meal, per child, but they have to go through a licensed sponsor in order to get reimbursed, someone who verifies all is in order. My wife or her workers will go in to make sure the daycares are feeding the kids the right foods at the right times. She examines their receipts and makes sure they are legitimate. She sends the accounting and paperwork to the government. The government pays her company, and she disburses it to the daycares. Her company makes a fee from this. So that's what Balanced Nutrition does.

* * *

At Davis Furniture, my job was very different from what I'd done before in furniture making. I was a material handler. I received material from trucks parked by the back door. I put those parts on the shelves where they needed to go, and then I took materials—covers, frames, all that good stuff—and lined it up for the upholsterers so that they could upholster the furniture. And once they upholstered the furniture, I took the furniture over to the other side, to shipping, assembly, or wherever it needed to go, and generally moved it through the value stream. Well, it wasn't called a value stream because they didn't do lean manufacturing, but that's how I thought of it. Through the stream.

It was a huge switch from Steelcase, which was one hundred

percent lean, to Davis, which was more like working in a furniture place in the 1980s.

* * *

While working at Davis, I was able to continue attending UNCG thanks to the company's willingness to bear with me on my schedule. I was blessed to have found another great job. Yolanda, too, had her new venture. We were finally on stable ground, and our family was healthy, happy, and growing as our daughter was married and starting her own family.

Adulthood is never easy, but the trials we experienced made us stronger. They matured us in our faith and our values. I am thankful that Yolanda and I have always been a team with a common goal and vision. We are still growing and maturing, a process that we know will never truly stop. I think back to when we were younger, earlier in our marriage, and how we were less firm in our stance on certain moral or political issues. But God used our experiences, both good and bad, to shape and chisel our convictions to be more in line with the principles of Scripture. He used those experiences to teach us to cry out to him for wisdom and guidance, and he has always been faithful to provide it.

* * *

Davis Furniture was entirely supportive of me. While I was there, I was also in school. I told them I was just going to be there while I was in college. I wanted to teach history. They let me schedule around my classes, and my boss was fine with my student schedule.

"As long as you got everything lined up, you're good to go."

I never had any complaints. The only time it got at all contentious at Davis was after the city council speech that changed—well, everything. There were days when my phone would not stop ringing, and people wanted to interview me for this and that. My boss finally sat me down and asked me what I wanted to do.

I reflected and realized he was right. I must choose. I may never have a chance to do something that has so much impact again. So I quit. There were no hard feelings at all. They told me that if I ever wanted my job back, it was open for me to return to. August 17, 2018, was my final day there.

Davis Furniture was the last place I worked for a wage before I entered politics. Of course, if the liberals and progressives manage to put all the conservatives in gulags for believing in seditious ideas like individual liberty and natural rights, I may have to go back and work there for free! Build that furniture! Send it to the Chinese!

Don't worry; we lovers of freedom are never going to let that happen.

I've been back several times since. I went back when I was on the campaign trail, then after I won the election. And I was there and spoke when they opened a new plant in High Point in June 2021. After I finished the ceremony, I went down to Plant Five where I used to work and talked to those guys who are employed there now. It was like coming home.

But I'm getting ahead of the story.

12

PRELUDE TO POLITICS

AT ST. STEPHEN CHURCH, we never talked about being "saved," even though I had heard the term. I didn't really understand what it meant. But one day in my early twenties, while I was in the reserves, going to (and washing out of) A&T, and working at Domino's, my best friend Wayne Campbell called me and told me about a church he'd been attending that met at NC A&T in the student union.

I'd met Wayne in the fourth grade, and we became friends in the fifth grade at Porter Elementary. We've been best buds ever since. Wayne had become saved before me. He'd grown up in church, as I had, but at A&T, he truly found the Lord.

He begged me to go with him.

I said no. I had a church, after all!

Wayne kept at me.

I finally relented, said all right, and went with Wayne.

That's the night I got saved and formed a personal relationship with Jesus.

I don't remember who was preaching. I don't remember much

beyond the profound, life-changing experience that I felt within. Now, as I've recounted, I didn't become a changed man overnight by any means. I still had a great deal of growing up to do.

I was still living with one foot in both worlds. But much as my political journey started shortly thereafter, that's where my spiritual journey started.

The same way I continued to grow politically, I continued to grow spiritually. Here's the odd thing: Wayne Campbell is the one who took me to that church where I got saved. He's also the one I had an argument with about Rush Limbaugh—an argument that started me on my political journey. Wayne's responsible for a lot. In fact, in a way, most of my spiritual and intellectual growth is due to Wayne Campbell.

Wayne now lives in Denton, Texas, by the way. I talk to him on the phone all the time and just saw him recently when I went to Dallas for an NRA board meeting.

* * *

My favorite part of attending St. Stephen Church was the music. They had a pipe organ and piano. Joyce McClain played the piano for many years, and she was wonderful. The organist and choir director was Geraldine Dillard. The choir was great. What I liked about our choir was that we sang traditional hymns. Every first Sunday, we'd sing "Amazing Grace" after communion. We sang "Holy, Holy, Holy" as the processional.

"God of Our Fathers," "How Great Thou Art."—I grew up listening to these standard hymns. But here's the thing: I would stand, hold the hymnal, but never make a sound. As I grew older, I'd listen to that music and loved it. I would stand beside my wife, my kids, and still not make a sound. I'd just read and listen to the music and enjoy it.

My mom became an accomplished singer in the choir once she started going. She had a fantastic voice. She was a soprano who sang solos, and she was known not just at our church but throughout the city. She'd been invited to sing at many events. But I didn't sing anything and never had. The closest I ever came was when my brothers, sisters, and I would sit in front of the stereo and sing along with rock and roll records.

But one day my wife and I were standing around after a church service, getting ready to go. The organist would play music as people were milling around until the sanctuary cleared out. She had just finished playing. I had been talking to several people and was still there. She called me up front. And as I walked up to the pulpit area, I assumed she was going to ask me where my mother was.

The organist's name was Mrs. Geraldine Dillard. Everybody referred to her as Sarge. She was quite the character. She called me up to the organ. She just looked at me. She didn't ask me how I was doing.

Sarge just looked at me and said, "You're Robinson, aren't you?"

I said, "Yes, ma'am."

She said, "Eva Robinson's son?"

I answered "yes" again.

She said, "You will come to choir practice Wednesday."

I'm thinking for *what*?

But I said, "Okay."

After that, I left. Usually when we left, we'd go over to my mom's house for a while, hang out, and let the kids stay there for a while. So I told my mom that Mrs. Dillard told me to come to choir practice.

She had the same reaction that I had. "For what? She wants you to sing in the choir?"

"I have no idea."

So that Wednesday I went to choir practice. I sat down.

Sarge looked at me and said, "Two Sundays from now, not this Sunday but the following Sunday, I need you to sing a solo."

My only thought was, "I don't sing. Who told you I sing? Are you crazy?"

But I shrugged, shook my head, and replied, "Okay. I don't know how it's going to come out, though."

She replied, "It'll come out fine; don't worry about it."

She gave me the song. It was "Great Is Thy Faithfulness." I listened to it that night. The men sang along to it. She made a recording of herself playing it on the piano and gave it to me on tape. I took that tape, put it in the car, and would drive down the street practicing. I'd listen and think to myself, "Nobody's going to like this. *I* don't like this. But Sarge wants me to do it, so I'm going to do it."

I told my mom about my assignment.

"Can you sing?"

"I've never tried."

She seemed very nervous about it. "I don't know how it's going to turn out."

Two weeks later, I'm in the choir room putting my robe on. All these men I practiced the song with are saying it's going to turn out great. I'm thinking, "No, it's not going to go well. Not well at all."

So out we come. The service started, and then it was time to sing the song. I was standing up with the choir, but a little separate for the solo. At St. Stephen, there are two choir areas, and we were on the main choir stand. The organist played the introduction, and I started to sing. And soon as I hit the first notes, I hear some "amens" from the congregation. What was going on?

I don't even really remember singing the solo. I just remember getting finished. And when I was finished, the whole place was standing up, clapping. My mom was out there, crying and carrying on along with them.

At the time, there was a man named Mr. Murphy who had once been the main male soloist in the church. He had died about a month or two before. After the service, people came to me saying, "Mr. Murphy just died, and now God has sent up somebody else to be our male soloist. It's amazing how God works."

I was thinking, "This is crazy. I ain't never sung anything before."

I continued to sing at our church. And before long, other churches asked me to come in and guest solo as well. I sang several cantatas at other churches for events for Easter and Christmas. And it continued like that for a number of years until we left St. Stephen for less secular, more spiritually nurturing pastures.

Once I left St. Stephen, I stopped singing in church. But I also started singing on my own, trying to develop my voice a little more to sing popular music. Then one evening, somebody heard me singing at work—this was at Steelcase—and the song they heard me singing was "You're a Mean One, Mr. Grinch."

They called people over and had me sing it again. "That's crazy! How do you do that? Sounds just like it should." One night we all went to karaoke, and a friend wanted me to sing "The Gambler," by Kenny Rogers. So I got up and did it, and the people in the audience went nuts. So I've done karaoke singing ever since. I get a kick out of it, and others seemed to like it.

During the campaign, because someone told somebody else that I could sing, I ended up singing at a church. I sang "Great Is Thy Faithfulness," I believe, and that video went semi-viral. That's how it got out to the general populace that I could sing.

Singing is not something I take very seriously, but there are people who like to hear me sing. I'm not against it. Singing in a church where I am speaking or visiting is by no means out of the question. I'll sing in church. When I really sing sincerely, it's going to be at church. I'm a bass or baritone normally, but I'll sing anything.

I like to trip people out by singing the song "Sukiyaki" in Japanese and performing it in a high register. People will ask "How are you making that sound come out of you when you talk so deep?"

Another high one I sang a lot at Steelcase was the Sam Cooke song "Chain Gang." It seems funny because I certainly look like a big bass singer, and hearing that high sound coming out somehow doesn't fit. "Nothing like that ought to be coming out of you," they'd say.

Oddly enough, I'm still not a big fan of sitting in the pews and singing in the congregation because now I feel like everybody's listening to me, and I still can't read music!

* * *

During the last term of Bill Clinton's presidency, I was at my mom's house one day when Wayne Campbell came over. We were not paying much attention to the television, but at some point Rush Limbaugh popped up on the screen. I turned around and saw him and commented, "Oh God, I can't stand that guy."

Wayne looked at me and said, "Well, why?"

I said, "Cause that dude, he's a racist, man. He's a bigot."

Wayne looked at me and said, "Do you know him?"

"No, I don't know him."

"Do you listen to his radio program?"

"No, I don't listen to his program."

"Do you read any of his books?"

"No, I do not."

"Then how do you know he's a racist?"

"Everybody on television and radio *says* he's a racist. That's why."

Now Wayne and I always talked about everything.

He said, "You told me one time that people on television characterize black people as thieves and liars who don't care for their children."

"Yes. So?"

"Well, if they are lying about black people, how do you know they're not lying about Rush Limbaugh?"

I was mad at Wayne for calling me out like that. I felt like he was tripping. Limbaugh *had* to be a racist—and I was going to go get Limbaugh's book, read it, and prove it to Wayne. I went and bought his book, and when I bought the book, I bought a highlighter too. I purchased them at a big bookstore in Golden Gate Shopping Center.

Boy, was I going to show Wayne.

The title of the book was *The Way Things Ought to Be*. I got that book, started reading it, and—*uh oh*.

The arguments and conclusions in that book were matters I'd been turning over in my mind since I was a kid. Reading Limbaugh reminded me of conversations that my siblings and I had had years ago when we were talking about what was right and wrong, fair and unfair.

I thought, "This is crazy. It's like this guy is inside my head." It really felt that way. "This jerk is stealing my ideas!"

By reading that book I discovered I was conservative—and always had been my whole life. I am not a Democrat who became a conservative Republican. Reading Rush Limbaugh's book did not change the way I thought. Instead, it helped me realize how to characterize the beliefs I already had.

The same applies to Yolanda. Both of us have always been conservative and Republican in outlook. Yolanda in fact, registered Republican when she first registered to vote. She's never voted for a Democrat. This is very much based on her religious views. She considers politics downstream from her faith.

After reading *The Way Things Ought to Be,* I went back and talked to Wayne. That's when he and I started getting involved with politics. I examined the differences between the two parties: what the Republican Party had done, what the Democratic Party had done, and the history of the Democratic Party. I looked at, really scrutinized, what both of them stood for then and stood for now. It was a logical choice for me to end on the Republican side. Republicans believe in everything I believe in and always have.

One of the misconceptions liberals and progressives have about me is that I don't like black people. "He doesn't like black people. He's a self-hater."

Nothing could be further from the truth.

The problem is that I am disgusted by people on the left who mischaracterize the story of black Americans. They take the story of black Americans and turn into a tale of "woe is me." All the movies that come out about the so-called black experience. My brother and I have a saying. "It's another Lord Have Mercy production of a Look How They Do Us Film."

It's disgusting when you take the story of people who have overcome so much, have been victorious over so much, have withstood the worst of times in this country, and have been at their absolute best at those worst of times, then try to turn it into this caricatured good-guy/bad-guy story, this "Woe is me. I'm just po' ole me, been chased by hounds and hit with water hoses Lord, have mercy."

That is not my story. That is not the story of black America. I say stop with that garbage. We have overcome. Our story is a story of survival and a story of victory. It's not a story of victimization and loss and despair.

The true story is about how people overcame, about how strong people were able to survive the worst of conditions in history and come out on top despite all that they faced. That's the story that I preach. That's the story that inspires me to be who I am. If I had to sum it up, that's the reason I'm a Republican. My beliefs grew out of my experience. They are not something I converted to. They are something I recognized that were already within me, that I grew up believing. It was a certainty that I could be anything I wanted to be, overcome anything I wanted to overcome.

Look through history. The Republican Party has stood up for things that I believe in for over a hundred years. They stood up for justice. They stood up for freedom. They stood up for equality. Years ago, they stood against slavery. Today they stand against abortion. Years ago, they stood for putting the Union back together and making it freer for everybody. Today they're standing up for the sovereignty of this nation, to keep it free and prosperous. They want to keep it together and keep it secure. You can go on and on down the list.

Detractors love to say the Republican Party changed. The Republican Party didn't change a thing. The Republican Party is still standing up and fighting for freedom and equality for everybody.

And the Democratic Party? The Democratic Party is still representing a bunch of wild-haired ideas that don't do anything but destroy a place. They believe in disregarding the law, disregarding common sense, and doing whatever their vaunted sense of justice tells them— which conveniently turns out to be whatever they want to do anyway. It's always been to the detriment of people, and it's always been to the detriment of this country. Black people were historically Republican but began to shift during the New Deal. They took a hard left turn in the 1960s, and it's been downhill since for black people.

I am not about defeat, so it was natural for me to fall on the right side of things.

Now I believe that I can be a part of pulling the cataracts off a lot of black people's eyes. The key to it is telling them the story of the Republican Party. And, most of all, sharing the true story of not being a victim.

You are not a victim forever. Have you been a victim of wrongdoing? Yes. But you were victorious over that. Somebody was victorious over that on your behalf. There's no reason for you to look at yourself in the mirror and think you are a victim. You're a receiver of benefits because of what people who came before you did. You should be a benefactor for others.

Go do it.

* * *

When George W. Bush was running for president, I first got involved in local politics. I was already engaged during 9-11, all through the Bush presidency, and into his second term. I went to party meetings, I got involved supporting candidates, and I spent time campaigning for them

Over time, though, I became disillusioned. The party at that point didn't want to fight. Anybody who was a fighter had been run out of the party, and they were a bunch of milquetoast sorts who just wanted to talk about lower taxes and less government. They didn't want to take on the issues the Democrats had assumed ownership of, the narratives they were skewing in order to get black folks to vote Democratic.

That's what I cared about the most, and Republicans at the time were scared to death to talk about any of it. I felt if they didn't want to talk about that, there was no reason for me to be there.

My attitude became, "I'm not going to waste time on this. You don't want to expand the party, so I'm not interested."

I decided I would go back to my normal life and try to tell people what I believed in my own manner.

I didn't abandon the Republican Party, but I wasn't going to go down there and listen to them talk about things that weren't going to draw anybody into the party. You must pull in new voters. You must if you want to stay viable. They were not doing it.

* * *

If you've heard anything about Greensboro, you've probably heard about the Woolworth sit-in—and you've heard of the so-called Greensboro massacre. This was actually a gunfight between the Klan and Communists in 1972. It was all motivated by money and a grab at power by the most misguided and amoral people in the American political arena, the American Communist Party.

Look at Bloody Sunday in Moscow in 1917. Soldiers shot all the people in the streets. It was clear to see what the Communists wanted, just as it was obvious what they wanted in 1972. They wanted to provoke the Klan by staging a protest in a black neighborhood. They were hoping the Klan would come down, possibly kill some folks, maybe kill some civilians standing nearby, or perhaps shoot some kid on his bicycle. They are that given to depraved utilitarian morality. And they could use such a thing as a rallying cry for the whole black community to join the Communist Party. They wanted to get the revolution jump-started in Greensboro.

It didn't work out that way. Black people are smarter than that. After it happened, most black people in the city were like, "Look, you can go find a field north of town and go shoot each other to pieces there. We want both of you out of our community." So at the time, it backfired.

But the ultra-left continued to live off this event and threatened the city for years. They wanted a plaque, an apology from the police. The city council had a meeting about it, and I went down.

That was the *first* time I spoke before the Greensboro City Council, and that was a speech I actually wrote. It was memorable for one reason: at the end of it, I said, "Y'all are trying to say that the city needs to heal from this shooting, to heal racially. I say the city is *already* healed. If you don't believe that, take a look at the mayor."

The mayor was a black woman at the time.

"They're standing there, telling us the city had to heal from all this animus between white and black. The city has elected a black female as mayor."

The whole thing was ridiculous.

Even before I was politically aware, I had the Communists' number. I began to understand what had happened in Vietnam in high school. Both of my JROTC instructors were Vietnam vets, and they told me about the purpose of the war, who was behind the Viet Cong and Viet Min, and what they really believed. I've been a virulent anti-communist since I was a teenager. I've understood the dreadful consequences of communism. Communists are easy to see through. They don't ever do anything new. Everything they do is from the same playbook. Each communist revolution is a mirror image of the others. Different people. Different places. Same playbook.

And what went on in Greensboro with the Klan? The Klan and racial animus were used by the Communist Party in North Carolina as a means to get a political foothold in this state. The Communists were going to point to the Klan and say, "The Klan is the bad guy; the Communist Party is the good guy."

The truth was, they were both bad guys.

They made the Klan their target because who doesn't want to beat up on the Klan, those horrible guys in bed sheets? They go around lynching people. So join the Communist Party! We're the only ones that have enough guts to fight these guys!"

So that was their move for political power. I never understood the point of the Greensboro Shootout until I really studied it for the city council speech. I found that first of all, the police had told the Communist leader Johnson and his crew: "Do *not* have this rally. Don't have it in *that* neighborhood. The Klan is going to show up. There's going to be trouble. Stop provoking these guys. These guys are dangerous."

The commies didn't listen to them. They wanted black people to be hurt.

Then I found out that the Klan wasn't the only group that had guns that day. The Communists had guns, too, and it's just as likely that they're the ones who fired the first shot.

The Klan was riding *through* the rally. These guys blocked them, kicked their cars, told them to get out, and challenged them to a fight. The Klansmen exited their vehicles unarmed. But once the Klansmen were confronted by the threat of a gun, they retrieved their own weapons. At that point, it became a gun fight—a gunfight that the commies lost. It was trouble all around. The fact that someone was killed was tragic. But the confrontation and aftermath were built on provocations and circumstances that easily could have been avoided.[1]

Should the Klan have been found guilty of murder? That's a matter for the courts. But in the court of public opinion it is undeniable that this fight was precipitated by the Communists. Of course, the Klan went too far. That's what they do. Just as the police told everyone they would. Just as everyone knew they would.

That's what precipitated my going to the meeting. I didn't see anybody trying to challenge these guys who wanted to commemorate this idiocy for something it was most emphatically *not*. They wanted the city of Greensboro to apologize for the shootings, and they were saying that Greensboro was *still* racist, that there were still hard feelings about this, and that the people of the city were crying out for justice.

What a load of nonsense.

I went to explain that nobody was crying out for justice here. The only people who are crying are you all, and the only reason that you're doing it is because you want money and power. The political organization that was pushing the whole thing was run by a man named Nelson

---

1   See Robert Watson's account in *Harper's Magazine*, March 1980. An excerpt can be found here: https://www.washingtonpost.com/archive/opinions/1980/03/02/the-other-side-of-the-greensboro-shootout/78eeddfa-820d-4100-ae8a-c085d548e0e7/

Johnson. He was the organizer of something called GAPP. Greensboro Association of Poor People.

Oddly enough, when I was a child, we used to go to something called the GAPP house. It was supposed to be a refuge for poor children like me to come to, where we could hang out, do homework, and get tutoring. But it wasn't that. It was a place where people came, smoked cigarettes, and talked about communism and revolution. And it was heavily involved in trying to recruit young people into the Communist Party. My brother and sister worked at the Pace Taylor YMCA, and their boss was deeply involved in that stuff. She was trying to get them both to come to that rally.

My sister Alice flat out said no. My brother Michael was going to go, but he overslept. I think my mom might have had something to do with that. It's hard to get Alice to do anything she doesn't want to do. My sister hated that lady. She couldn't stand her.

So years later, that's how I came to give that speech. That was before Facebook and the internet—the Ancient of Days.

So I actually had given a speech before the Greensboro City Council before my speech on the Second Amendment in 2018. That's part of the reason that, when I got up to there the second time, I said, "I didn't have time to write a speech."

Because the first time, I did. I took a day or two to write the previous speech. I had it on the little index cards and went up there and delivered it. Nobody much cared. The idiots got their plaque and unnecessary apology.

The second time I didn't. This was one of the reasons I hadn't wanted to go. I hadn't prepared anything. But one thing was different—me. I was a much sharper weapon. I had been whetted and honed through the rough and tumble environment of social media. I had put in *years* of Facebook argumentation and meme making.

I had been in the fire, getting ready. And let me tell you, there are no fires hotter than the fires of social media.

13

MAKING MEMES

DECEMBER OF 2007 was when I joined Facebook. When I first went on, I did so for one reason and one reason only: to talk about professional wrestling. And the first post I ever put up was about professional wrestling. I think I put something about Lewis R. "Freight Train" Jones. That's all I did for a while. I did it with a friend of mine, Matt Swopes. We would exchange jokes about Andre the Giant and Rufus Jones and Dusty Rhodes. Silliness.

But I kept encountering people talking about politics online, and sometimes bringing it to my page. I knew a thing or two about politics at that point. I knew Republicans and Democrats, who the candidates were, and what the issues were. People would say things that were stupid or wrong. I wouldn't insult them, but I would reply, "No, that's not how that happened," trying to instruct more than contradict. I'd write a long explanation of what happened, as politely as I could, and when it didn't go along with the Democratic narrative, I got called names, Uncle Tom and the like. I would get a lot of "I can't believe you believe this" responses.

I'd come back with, "There's no use to call names; this is the truth. Go look it up." I tried to be reasonable, but of course that proved to be impossible. I quickly learned that people had no interest in moderation on social media.

Finally, it got to the point where somebody did some dumb political name-calling against me, and I decided I wasn't taking it anymore. I erased everything else, and I made my page all political.

Every political thought I had in my head, I put on there, up to and including my posting photos of Martin Luther King and calling him a communist. He was, of course, whatever else he did. History is what was, not what you wish were true. I didn't hold back anything. I wanted to be as demonstrative as possible because I wanted people to, as the guy said, "Come at me, bro." I wanted people to come at me. I wanted to be as in their faces as possible. I wanted people to read my page and go "*What* did he say? Did he *really* say that?" And that's what happened.

People would come to my page and challenge me over one thing or another. But I made nothing up. Every post was rooted in truth.

I remember somebody put up some dumb saying or meme: "One thing that can never be said is that a white person risked his life for a brown person." Some idiocy like that.

"Oh, I guess you don't know about William Lloyd Garrison, the editor of the *Liberator*." This man had to go live in a cave because he was writing an abolitionist newspaper."

I named him, I named Branch Rickey. I named a whole host of people fighting for black rights, for standing against slavery, against Jim Crow. I listed them. People enjoyed that post.

The first time I made a big splash on Facebook was during the Michael Brown and Ferguson controversy. I made a post that starts out "soft-headed negroes . . ."

I can't believe it's still up there. I'm surprised Facebook hasn't purged it. This post was shared many, many times. It started on July 8, 2016. I was in my bathroom at the rental house at Sassafras Court when I wrote this post. I wasn't going, but sitting on the closed toilet with my pants pulled up, thinking. And I wrote this post. Typed it on my phone.

Before I published it, I thought "Should I put that up?" and I answered, "Yeah, post it. Post it because I feel it." I felt it. So I posted it. Here it is.

* * *

You soft-headed Negroes who still think this is about "race" and "cops shooting black men" are blind. You are as blind as the Negroes who sold captives to Muslims on their caravans, and Europeans on their ships, instead of banding together to purge them from your land. You are as blind as the Negroes who allowed a party that hates you to buy your votes and loyalty for the right to live in the ghetto on welfare. You are as blind as the Negroes who sit and listen to a black man preach "black power" on white man's TV station that promotes the WORST of your people. And you are as blind as the Negroes who bemoan about "white privilege" while voting for a rich white woman who is brazenly flaunting her privilege IN YOUR FACE, by breaking a law that would put YOU under the jail, while she walks away without a slap on the wrist.

You need to close your mouths, open your eyes, and realize that this is only part of the devil's plan, not to destroy black people, or white people . . .

but ALL people.

* * *

I had been making Facebook posts and memes for almost ten years when I sat down to write my "soft-headed Negroes" post. I had collected maybe a thousand followers and was having a wonderful time expressing myself among likeminded people who were as fed up as I was at having to swallow the kind of junk out there passing for "official" black opinion. I knew that not only was I expressing positions that the vast majority of people supported, but I was expressing positions that the vast majority of *black* people supported. We were the majority.

Suddenly, my little post was all over the internet. It was popping up everywhere. People were claiming they wrote it, and I said, "You didn't write it; I did."

Now at the time, my mother had recently died, and I had put her photo up on my Facebook page as a tribute. It was the profile picture. I wanted people to see her on their feeds. People thought a woman had written the post. To this day, people think this—even though my name was on it. That was when I started to collect a lot of followers, five or six thousand. It stayed that way for a while. Then other posts went viral. I began to create memes. I loved doing that.

Over the years, I watched as the leftist agenda played out on our TV screens and social media. In 2012, Trayvon Martin, a young black man, was shot and killed in Sanford, Florida. In 2014, Michael Brown was shot and killed by a police officer in Ferguson, Missouri. In each of these events, false narratives of racism and police brutality were widely spread by the left. I was frustrated and vocal about it, especially on social media. I gained thousands of followers as I expressed my thoughts and opinions on these and other controversial topics. I was surprised, as I posted my hard-hitting thoughts on "black lives matter" and "hands up, don't shoot," how many Americans, liberal and conservative, black and white, embraced my message.

My social media page became a scrolling marquee of bold, unapologetic political commentary. I was growing adept at defending and debating my political position with those who disagreed. But that was from behind a screen. Of course, I didn't limit the expression of my opinions to typing on a screen only. I spoke out in person, too, but that was typically around my like-minded conservative friends or my family at the dinner table. I was comfortable with the 15,000 people who chose to follow me on social media, or the friends and family I knew would agree with and affirm my political positions. So to say that I was looking for the perfect opportunity to stand up and speak in front of a group of people who would oppose me could not be further from the truth.

In response to the Louisville, Kentucky, police raid where Breonna Taylor, girlfriend of the drug-dealing target of the raid, was shot by Officer John Mattingly, I created this meme:

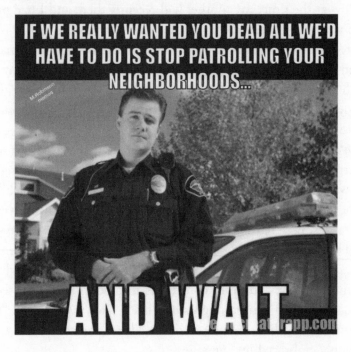

I made the meme sitting in a Cracker Barrel while eating breakfast. It was on a Fourth of July break from Davis. It went viral.

I have memes on Facebook that have 500,000 or more shares, organic shares off the page.

And some of these started getting media attention even back then. The "If we really wanted you dead" meme incensed many leftists by speaking the truth: cops are the best protection for many from the cancerous violence that engulfs some black communities. Of course, it was called racist. Of course, the opposite is the truth. If ever there were a non-racist meme about cops, this is it.

A correctional officer posted the meme and lost his job because of it. This led to a Kentucky television station running a story on it. They called in some expert who said, "It is obvious that whoever made this is a middle-aged white male, probably disgruntled by the changes in society, blah, blah, blah."

My wife showed me this report, and I called the news station. I told them I was the guy who created it. They seemed giddy with excitement and asked me questions. They wanted my name. I told them my name is right there on the corner of it. I sign my memes "M. Robinson Memes."

"Where are you from?" They were set to send someone to interview me.

I was really throwing on the Southern accent at that point, I have to admit. They got all excited, smelled a hit piece. They were super-excited until I said, "Oh, and by the way, I'm a black man."

"W-what?"

"I'm black."

"Are you serious?"

"Yes. I'm also a conservative. Been a conservative all my life."

"Oh . . . um, yeah. Let me get with my boss . . ."

Never heard from that reporter again.

They thought they had somebody they could hook to a post and whip, but nope.

Full disclosure: I don't read a lot of other people's opinions. Most of my reading is history, which I love. I do a lot of deducing.

In fact, true crime deduction shows are one of my favorite types of entertainment! I love *Forensic Files*, for instance. They'll start out with something like, "So-and-so was a vibrant member of the community until their body was found in a field, decomposed. Investigators are at a dead end. But a wad of chewed chewing gum and the imprint of a dog's behind will lead to the solution and reveal a terrible secret." And then, sure enough, the imprint of a dog's butt and a wad of chewing gum will solve the case.

Before I make public statements, I do a lot of checking. I go back and I check textbooks, historical records, and sources to make sure I have the facts straight, but that's the extent of it. I want names, dates, and historical occurrences; then I form my own thoughts. That's how I go about it. I don't read other people's thoughts on the matter, particularly contemporary opinions. I have enough of my own. Most of the time, when I think of an idea or a post or a meme, it comes from internal inspiration. I pull them out of I don't know where. I'll be walking along, and I'll think of something, and I'll say, "Oh, that'll make a good meme!"

I did a lot of that when I was at Davis Furniture. I'd have my phone in my pocket, and I'd be making a meme while walking around on breaks. I used two apps called PicCollage and Meme Generator a great deal. PicCollage is all I use now. I'm still making memes, but these days it's a lot sillier material. I like to take a break and have fun with them. I do Twitter now, and my Twitter account has gone way up, but most of my original posts are still on Facebook.

I did a bunch of posts and memes on the Obamas and on Michelle Obama, and some people don't like them.

Let me tell you something, I'm in the public eye now. I don't care what anybody says about me. If they are a private citizen and call me fat, black, and ugly, I don't care. If a private citizen on, say, his Twitter page, wants to call me names, more power to them. It's their right, just as it was mine as a private citizen to make fun of public officials and those who seek to be before the public eye. Michelle Obama was a person serving in an official government capacity, making speeches and appearances where she expressed political opinions backed up by the weight of her official position. She was doing public relations, appearing on magazine covers—plus she was married to the most public citizen in the world, the president of the United States, and she was and is a politician herself. I was a private citizen. I had the right to say whatever I wanted to say about her.

We used to burn politicians in effigy. Today we do it on Facebook and on Twitter. This is no different from what we did in the past. It is political expression. As long as I'm not threatening to kill her or making some kind of physical threat—and we all know what those would be; it's common sense—there's not a thing in the world wrong with making fun of Michelle Obama's pomposity or anyone else's or making fun of the media's obsession with the appearance of somebody who is, one must admit, a very ordinary-looking person. She's criticizing her fellow Americans loudly and publicly. I, as one she affronted, called her names right back.

Michelle Obama said some very disturbing things about this country, very disturbing indeed. She stood on stage and said *for the first time in her life* she was proud to be an American—these words are insulting to those who have done so much, achieved so much. It makes me want to say something equally ugly in their defense, in my defense. And as a private citizen, that's exactly what I did.

Now I did draw a line when it comes to children. I never would post anything about the Obama children, or about their family in general. But the two of them, Michelle and Barack Obama? I used to give them holy hell and say some very mean things about them. This is the nature of American political discourse. Again, I was a private citizen. I wasn't threatening to do them any harm. Most of what I said was in jest, and a large portion of it was political jabs, like a political cartoon, just done in a different format. If people don't like it, that's too bad. I got some tissue for them if they go to crying.

Of all the posts I ever made on social media, there's only one I wish I had worded differently. It's this one:

> It is absolutely AMAZING to me that people who know so little about their true history and REFUSE to acknowledge the pure sorry state of their current condition can get so excited about a fictional "hero" created by an agnostic Jew and put to film by a satanic Marxist. How can this trash, that was only created to pull the shekels out of your Schvartze pockets, invoke any pride?

I made that post when the movie *Black Panther* came out. I was very frustrated because there were so many black people who came up to me and said things like, "Oh, *Black Panther* is *sooo* motivating to black people."

And I'm like, "Guys, you do realize, number one, that Wakanda or whatever . . . that's *not even a real place*? This is a cartoon movie, for crying out loud! This is not something to be running around beating your chest talking about and exclaiming how proud it makes you feel. You do know who made it and what he said about the movie, right? Come on, this is Hollywood, guys. Get your heads out of your butt."

So that was the point of that post. What I should have done was find the real quote from Mel Brooks that I was referring to. It probably would have been next to impossible because it was something I remember as being on *Entertainment Tonight* from the 1980s. But I should have put that quote on it instead of my paraphrase. I heard him say one time that when you make a movie, you have to know who your audience is. Mel Brooks said if you want to get the shekels, you got to know who you are playing to. And I heard Mel Brooks, well known for doing humor from a Jewish perspective, saying that. That's what I put in the post, the comment about the shekels.

The point was this: "Look, these people in Hollywood, they're just after your money. They don't care anything about promoting you as being great people. They want your money. They're going to do whatever they can to get your money." As far as the guy being an agnostic Jew, that's how he described himself. He described himself using just those words.

People took it the wrong way, and I can see why people took it the wrong way. It came off the wrong way. When people called me and asked about it, that's what I told them. And I apologized to them.

It's the only time I've ever apologized for anything I put on Facebook. It did come out wrong. I knew the truth of what I was trying to say, but I should have chosen different words. I was very angry at myself for doing that too. I'm usually very, very careful about what I write on Facebook, even though when I write forcefully, it might not seem like it sometimes. But I am very careful about what I write, and at that moment I was wrong.

Who stands up for Jewish people in this day and age? Look at the vile anti-Semitism perpetrated on the streets of Los Angeles in 2021, antifa thugs physically attacking Jewish people for wearing a yarmulke? Look at Israel facing Palestinian rocket and terrorist attacks on the lives of the people. Who stands up? The Republican Party, that's who. The Democratic Party is a home to anti-Semites. There's no doubt about that.

Jewish people, like black people, are starting to wake up to this, but it's taking a long time and harm is being done. I have made a friend because of this Facebook post, a rabbi. We talked, and he said he felt he and I were in a way stuck in the same situation because we're surrounded by people, those we love, who are doing things to hurt themselves, which is to continually vote for the Democratic Party.

Anyway, I don't fault anybody for being upset about that post. It didn't convey what I was trying to say.

When it comes to posts on Facebook, you have to be calculating. You can't just post willy-nilly. You must watch your words to keep from being thrown in Facebook jail. Last time I was thrown in Facebook jail, it was because I put up a post on April Fool's Day that said "I'm looking to trade all my guns for some good vegan cookbooks, or some good vegan recipes. Inbox me." It was a total joke, but they put me in Facebook jail for several days. So because I choose to keep using the platform, I'm careful about what I say.

More importantly, I choose my words in order to sway people. I try to do what I call "bulletproof writing." I try to think ten steps ahead of people who will oppose or argue with what I'm saying and include a response in the post. Here's how you know when it works: the first person who opposes or doesn't agree with you replies with an insult, calls you a "racist bastard," or curses you out instead of making a decent response. That's when you know you won. When calling me a vile name or telling me to go perform an unnatural act is all they can say, then victory is mine. I throw my hands up like Rocky.

14

FORTY YEARS OF FRUSTRATION

SO THERE IT WAS: a Facebook post from a friend of mine about teaching his son to shoot a rifle. The rifle was an AR-15, with all the trimmings.

I wanted a rifle like that. First I wanted it because, as you may have noticed, I love technology, love machinery that does what it's supposed to do in a cool or elegant way. Second, as you've seen, I have a history with rifles and rifle lore, both in the Army and in JROTC. And third, I wanted it because it was my right under the United States Constitution to have one. I have a right to bear arms, primarily as a defense against a tyrannical government, but also for self-defense. The two go hand in hand. The Second Amendment of the US Constitution is merely delineating a right we already possess. It's pointing this right out, not creating it.

And I wanted to *exercise* that right. I wanted to own a rifle like that.

I asked around about how to get a tricked-out AR-15 like my friend's.

Everybody recommended the upcoming Greensboro Gun Show as the place to get what I really wanted at a decent price, along with some expert advice on how to put it all together.

I was excited. I was going to get a rifle again. Heck, maybe next I would go to a violin show and get a violin to round out the things I missed from my youth!

"Greensboro City Council to cancel annual gun show."

Oh, man.

On February 14, a few weeks before, a disturbed young man had killed seventeen students at Marjory Stoneman Douglas High School in Parkland, Florida. He'd done it during a mass shooting with an AR-15 type rifle.

Now the Greensboro City Council in North Carolina wanted to cancel our gun show because of something that happened hundreds of miles away and had nothing to do with us.

Was I surprised?

Of course not. This was just another episode of left-wing fanatics trying to use personal tragedy and the criminal acts of one individual to destroy their political opposition. And the political opposition was *me*—a law-abiding American, a man with full rights under the United States Constitution.

What had I done wrong? Nothing. What had that gun in Florida done wrong, for that matter? Nothing. It was the disturbed killer who had perpetrated this evil act. There is evil in the world. Satan is real, and he's after us; make no mistake. He must be opposed. But evil doesn't reside in the "system" or in inanimate objects. Evil resides in the individual heart.

Those people, like members of the city council, who want to shut down gun shows and limit gun rights are fighting *for* evil, not against it. They are aiding and abetting criminals so they can go up against an unarmed, helpless population.

I was so mad. More than mad. It struck at my understanding of myself as an American. I was a law-abiding man who was looking forward to purchasing a rifle at this gun show.

I drove to work that day frustrated as I thought about how the leftist gun control narrative had now come to my hometown.

I posted about this on social media. But somehow, this time it didn't feel like *enough*. Forty years of frustration came bubbling up. We the people have individual rights. We are not the sum total of any identity group, any race or creed. We are individuals first and foremost. And it seemed like the previous four decades in America had consisted of a steady exercise of grinding down the individual in favor of some spurious group or another. The right to bear arms had lately been under the most furious attack.

For a moment, I thought we were going to get a reprieve when the city attorney told the council that if they cancelled the show, they could be sued, and more penalties could be involved.

The city council didn't care. They were on their progressive high horse. They were going to punish the "gun nuts."

I knew the meeting that evening would be packed with the local activist crowd. The students would stir up fear that "gun violence" was about to hit the local universities and schools.

I need to go, I kept thinking to myself. *I need to go.*

I had to work until 4:30 that day, and the 5:30 meeting was sure to be packed. Maybe I should skip it and post something on Facebook instead.

"What are you going to do about it?" a friend asked me. "All you can do is talk. Those people are going to do whatever they want to do, and there's nothing you can do about it."

I looked at him and said, "Just talk? You know the American Revolution didn't start with that shot heard round the world. It started with talking, with someone asking, 'Why can't we be free?'"

I walked away from my friend and went straight to the restroom. I closed the door, looked at myself in the mirror, and thought, *You gotta go to that meeting. You have to so you can live with yourself. You know what you believe.*

When I left that restroom, I knew I was going to the meeting.

I left work, went home to quickly grab a bite to eat, told my wife where I was going, and headed to the city council meeting. I was nervous in the car. This was different. I wasn't talking to my conservative friends or dictating my opinions to those who agreed with me. I wasn't sitting in the comfort of my home, typing political commentary from behind the safety of a screen. Yes, this was going to be very different.

I arrived and took a seat among all the other citizens there. I heard one stupid, leftist argument after another. It was like they were pounding on the stupid.

The meeting was supposed to address gun violence as it related to whether or not Greensboro should host this gun show, but people kept saying things that had nothing to do with that subject. There was a great deal of identity politics flying around. Some were making dumb jokes such as, "Big Glocks, small . . . brains," in the middle of a serious governmental meeting.

I sighed in disgust. It was so ridiculous and demeaning.

I knew I had to speak. Someone had to make some sense!

One speaker after another had been talking about "minority rights" this, and "minority rights" that.

Someone had to speak for the majority.

I realized that—at this time, in this place—that someone had to be me.

15

I AM THE MAJORITY

PUBLIC COMMENT DELIVERED BEFORE THE
CITY COUNCIL OF GREENSBORO ON APRIL 3, 2018

"I DIDN'T HAVE TIME to write a fancy speech, I didn't have time to, you know, I didn't have the resource of an English teacher to sit down and write a speech with at school today, to be brought over here or to practice or anything. What I really came down here for is this: I've heard a whole lot of people in here talking tonight about this group and that group, domestic violence and blacks, these minorities and that minority. What I want to know is, when are you all going to start standing up for the majority? And here's who the majority is: I'm the majority. I'm a law-abiding citizen who's never shot anybody, never committed a serious crime, never committed a felony. I've never done anything like that. But it seems like every time we have one of these shootings, nobody wants to put the blame where it goes, which is at the shooter's feet. You want to put it at my feet. You want to turn around and restrict my constitutional right that's spelled out in black and white. You want to restrict my right to buy a firearm and protect myself from some of the very people you're talking about in here tonight. It's ridiculous. I don't think Rod Serling could come up with a better script.

It does not make any sense. The law-abiding citizens of this community and many communities around this country, we're the first ones taxed, and the last ones considered, and the first ones punished when things like this happen because our rights are the ones being taken away. That's the reason why I came down here today. Gun show or no gun show, NRA or no NRA, I'm here to stand up for the law-abiding citizens of this community. Because I'm going to tell you what's going to happen. You can take the guns away from us all you want to. You all write a law; I follow the law, I'll bring my guns down here, I'll turn them in. But here's what's going to happen. The Crips and the Bloods on the other side of town, they're not going to turn their guns in. They're going to hold on to them. And what's going to happen when you have to send the police down there to go take them?

The police can barely enforce the law as it is. And from what I see, we demonize the police, criminalize and vilify the police, and we make the criminals into victims. And we're talking about restricting guns? How are you going to do that? How are you going to do that when the police department is already hamstrung? You're not going to be able to go down here and take these guns from these criminals. So the criminals are going to hold on to their guns. They're still going to have them. They're still going to break into my house, and they're still going to shoot me with them. And guess who's going to be the one that suffers? It's going to be me.

Well, I'm here to tell you tonight, it is not going to happen without a fight. And when I say fight, I don't mean shots fired, I don't mean fists thrown. I mean I'm going to come down here to this city council and raise hell, just like these loonies from the left do, until you listen to the majority of the people in this city. And I am the majority. The majority of the people in this city are law-abiding, and they follow the law, and they want their constitutional right to be able to bear arms. They want to be able to go to the gun show and buy a hunting rifle or sport rifle. They're no military-grade weapons sold at the gun show. An AR-15 is not a military-grade weapon.

Anybody that would go into combat with an AR-15 is a fool. It's a semi-automatic .22 rifle. You'd be killed in fifteen minutes in combat with that thing. So we need to dispel all these myths, and we need to drop all this division we've got going on here. Because the bottom line is, when the Second Amendment was written, whether the framers liked it or not, they wrote it for everybody. And I am everybody. And the law-abiding citizens of this city are everybody. And we want our rights, and we want to keep our rights. And, by God, we are going to keep them, come hell or high water."

16

THE AFTERMATH

I WAS FINISHED. There was nothing more to say. I wanted to get out of the room as soon as possible. My emotions were bubbling at the surface, and I was still angry about all I had heard that night. I didn't need a confrontation with anyone at that time; I didn't want to say anything inappropriate in the heat of the moment.

As I turned to walk away from the podium, I saw a lady standing up. She was clapping excitedly. It was obvious she liked what I had said. And she wasn't alone. Several others were standing and clapping as well. But before I made it to the door, a young man made a ridiculous comment to me about the Constitution. I responded, "Son, you need to be quiet. You need to go back to school and get off Facebook and pick up a history book." I walked through the door without saying another word. I had only taken a few steps when six police officers started walking toward me. I asked myself, "Am I about to get arrested?" But then each one of them, one after the other, grabbed my hand to shake it and said, "Thank you, thank you." Then a lady from a radio station, I don't even know which one, interviewed me. Finally, I left the building.

When I got to my car, I was still so wound up I couldn't drive. I walked around my car three or four times to calm down before I was finally able to leave for home. By the time I arrived home, I felt like I had come down off the high.

I walked in the door, and Yolanda started the conversation, "How was the meeting?"

"It was fine."

"Well, what happened?"

"I don't know."

"What do you mean you don't know? Did you speak?"

"Yeah."

"What did you say?"

"I don't know."

At that point, I really could not remember anything I had said. It was such a blur. While driving home, I tried to remember, and when I got home, I was still trying to remember. I went on the website to see if I could view the video replay of the meeting, but it wasn't uploaded yet.

Yolanda asked me again what I had said, and I just shook my head.

"Was it good or bad?" she asked as she fished for more information.

"I don't know, but if the police show up, you might need to tell them I'm not home." I then recounted to her that several policemen actually shook my hand in gratitude. "And I did a radio interview with some lady," I continued.

"Well, it must have been good if you did a radio interview," she concluded.

"I know it sounds crazy, but I truly don't remember."

My wife kept trying to pry information out of me, but the whole thing was like a fuzzy dream. We were sitting in the living room when the Fox8 ten o'clock news came on. I couldn't believe it. I saw—and heard—myself on television: "Gun show or no gun show, NRA or no NRA, I'm here to stand up for the law-abiding citizens of this community."

Immediately the phone rang. It was a friend of Yolanda's, and I could hear her through the phone asking if that was me on the local news.

"I cannot believe this! I have to see this speech you made," my wife kept repeating.

"I'm sure they will have it on the website soon. You can probably see it tomorrow night."

We didn't have to wait that long. I went to work the next day, and one of my friends said, "Hey man, I saw that speech you gave. Man, that was good, that was really good." Then I checked social media on my phone, and I had a bunch of messages. "That speech was on fire!" "That was a great speech!" "Great speech, man!" I wondered how in the world people had seen it. Then I noticed a link they were referring to and clicked on it. A couple of members from Grassroots North Carolina, a Second Amendment advocacy group, had been present and had spoken at the city council meeting. They obtained the video of my speech that night and posted it to social media. I called my wife and told her that if she checked out Grassroots NC, she would be able to see and hear the speech there, since I had been of no help retelling it to her the night before. She quickly called me back: "Baby, that was *good!*"

After work, I went out to grab something to eat. I was on the way home when my wife called to say, "You will never guess who just called."

"Who?" I asked.

"Congressman Mark Walker . . . he shared your video and wants to meet you." All I could say was "Wow" and hung up. She called me right back and said, "You're not going to believe this. *Fox and Friends* just called, and they want you to be on the news."

"No, that's somebody playing a joke," I said.

"No, it's not." she responded. "They said they want you to go to a place they'd reserved for an interview."

That was not a calm evening at home. The phones did not stop. People were calling me, calling my wife, sending messages. The number of calls increased exponentially—all because the video of my speech was spreading. The meeting took place on Tuesday, April 3. On April 6, I appeared on *Fox and Friends*. They sent a car to pick me up and drove me to Winston-Salem, to the medical center, where they have an office to record live videos for national news.

I went in, and they miked me up, put makeup on me, and had me ready. Before the interview, I checked my social media page. I had 15,500 followers at that moment. I turned off my phone and did the interview on *Fox and Friends*. It was the very first national television interview I had ever done. I was still wound up tight about the whole thing. And when they asked me questions, I fired back. It was not a typical interview, but they loved it nonetheless. People were calling into the news station, trying to find out information about me. One of the cohosts of *Fox and Friends* was the first person to suggest I should run for office.

Run for office? I thought. *That sounds crazy.* I wasn't looking to do anything like that, but I had a really good experience with *Fox and Friends*.

Once the interview was over, I left the office and got on the elevator. It still seemed like a dream. Earlier that week I hadn't thought one bit about making a speech, much less being interviewed by Fox. I never would have imagined any of this. I turned my phone back on while on the elevator. By the time I got in the car, the number of my social media followers had doubled, jumping to 30,000. Little did we know that this was just the beginning. That night, my wife and I took a step back to ask ourselves, "What will this lead to? Is this going to come to an end soon, or is this just getting started?" We settled in after those three crazy days to prepare for where this might be taking us.

It wasn't long before the mailbox began to be filled with letters from across the country. I received mail from Washington, California, New York, Florida, and everywhere in between. They all had a similar theme.

"You spoke my mind."

"You said exactly what I think."

"You are the patriot we need in this country."

These people who wrote to me didn't really know me or know any other positions I held or how I thought about any other political topic. I remember one person who wrote to me saying, "You have to be a conservative because no one else would think like that except a conservative. That's how conservatives think."

The mail continued pouring in, the phone calls did not stop, and I was receiving emails as well. I had become a sort of celebrity overnight just for speaking my mind. But people say what they think all the time, especially nowadays on social media. I was one of those normal people who put his opinion out there on social media. What made this speech at a small city council meeting so different? I knew the majority of people in this country felt the same way I did. But sometimes, with the leftist media always in your face and the loudest voices belonging to those who oppose conservative values, it's easy to become disillusioned. All of these calls, letters, and emails were reminding me who the majority really was.

It wasn't long before the National Rifle Association (NRA) contacted me. They had watched my speech. In fact, I found out the folks at their offices had gathered together to watch the video and decided they must contact me. It turned out they wanted me to be in a commercial for them. We made plans to shoot the commercial in Greensboro at Center City Park. I met them there early one morning. They didn't have a script, per se, but rather some questions they wanted me to answer. They took that informal interview and put together the commercial they wanted. It was a fantastic experience, but even then, I did not realize how this would turn out to be the next big step of a journey.

Shortly after the commercial, the NRA invited us to attend their 2018 annual meeting in Dallas, Texas. The NRA flew us to Dallas, picked us up from the airport, and took us to our hotel. We met Wayne LaPierre, the chief executive and executive vice president of the NRA. We also met NASCAR legend Richard Childress, then an NRA board member. We had an amazing time encountering many great people.

One event of the NRA annual meeting is the Leadership Forum of the Institute for Legislative Action (ILA), an arm of the NRA. They informed me that they were planning to play the video of my speech at the Greensboro City Council to the assembled audience and also present me with a lifetime NRA membership.

President Trump spoke at that event. I was in the back in the "green room." I was very excited because I thought I was going to meet the president or at least see him. But when we went back, we were told we couldn't leave; the place was on lockdown because—you guessed it—the president was there. So I got to sit in the back in the green room and watch the president on a screen. Very anticlimactic, I have to say.

But once the president finished speaking and left the stage, they took me out onto the stage. A bunch of people in the audience went crazy with cheering and carrying on. I went out and gave a speech. Then they presented me with my lifetime membership.

They played the video of the speech.

The speaker came to the microphone, "How great is Mark Robinson?"

The people answered with continued applause. "Give me a little bit more, because if you want to hear from him, let's bring him out. Mark Robinson!"

Now, when I *was* asked to attend this meeting and told I would be receiving an award, I figured I would have to say a few words of thanks. I expected to walk up on stage, say a couple of words, accept the lifetime membership, shake a hand, and go back to my seat. But there I was, behind the microphone, listening to their applause and realizing that they wanted more than just a "Thanks for your kind applause."

They wanted to hear what I had to say. Again I found myself thinking, "I don't have a speech prepared." But by now a lifetime of experience had primed me for this moment. The applause died down, the audience went quiet, and it was time for me to speak. As I started talking, my thoughts were clear, and they flowed out confidently.

I began to realize that maybe I did have a knack for public speaking. It was a great night, a memory I will always cherish.

I had no idea where this was going, but I had the feeling that it was like a social media trend. I'd seen those happen on social media a lot. I figured it would go up, up, up, and then just wither away after a while. But it never has. It's just continued to go on and on—maybe because my original speech wasn't just a shot in dark. There was substance behind it.

When I left the convention, I felt like that would be it. I would go back to my normal life. People were going to forget about this. It would be like something I posted on my Facebook page, and someone might come across it later and think, "Oh look, it got a million views on Facebook back in the day."

But the effect of that speech did not dissipate.

17

FALSE STARTS AND BABY STEPS

WE ATTENDED the remaining events of the annual meeting and convention and returned home. They posted the video of me speaking there, and it went semi-viral. Soon more media outlets were calling me, wanting an interview. I was contacted by media outlets from across the country, both radio and television. A lot of these were people in the gun community: people with blogs, people with small radio shows.

Everything was so unexpected and surreal, but wonderful. My wife and I figured things would start to calm down around then. The weeks after that first speech had been a whirlwind of activity. But we assumed that, like with most things, the social media craze would pass, and the public would latch on to the next big thing. Our story would dwindle in views and posts, and life could go back to normal. But after the NRA event, we saw even more mail stack up, more phone calls, and more offers to speak at this rally or that rally. My wife began keeping my calendar and scheduling my speaking events. Before long, my schedule was planned out through the end of 2018.

I was invited to speak at gun rallies and political events. I was becoming a household name inside the community of gun owners and Second Amendment supporters across the nation.

But outside of that community, not so much. I was somewhat recognized locally in the political arena but by no means nationwide. Yolanda and I began to wonder what would become of this. Was an elected office in my future? My decision to go speak at that city council meeting was never intended to be the springboard into public service, but would it be? Was that what we wanted?

These questions and others ran through our minds. By August of 2018, my calendar had become so full of travel that I had to quit my manufacturing job. The management at Davis Furniture was gracious and supportive of me, both during my time in school and with the chaotic schedule I faced during this uncharted time. Of course, a packed travel schedule also meant that my pursuit of a history degree would have to be put on hold. I stopped three classes short of my degree. That is something I plan to complete, come hell or high water.

I had no idea what awaited me around the next bend in the road, but I knew I would not be able to devote the necessary time and energy to my classes that semester.

Then we followed some bad advice and made a mistake.

* * *

I was approached by a person who told me I should start a nonprofit that would highlight many conservative issues, not just gun rights. They told me it would be a way to continue to travel and speak—and also make money and support myself while doing this.

My wife and I decided to start a nonprofit called Majority Matters. We worked hard with it, but honestly there was something that just did not feel right. I hired an assistant, and we had a small board of directors, along with a few benefactors. We were raising a little money.

But I didn't like it.

I didn't like doing that almost from the start.

I was also involved with people I didn't particularly like. They were too concerned with making money and too concerned with making a name for themselves. Some of these were guys who bragged about walking into a police station with a loaded AR-15 simply because it was legal to do so.

I suppose it is legal to take a hammer and break every bone in my other hand, but why would I want to? Or to take a saw and cut my foot off? I won't be charged with a crime for doing that. But why would I want to? It's foolishness. People who pull such stunts are out to promote themselves, and they are always discussing money. It was always about making more of it and never about the real cause of preserving freedom. I suppose they might have wondered why I never talked to them again. I wasn't in this to get rich.

In order to make Majority Matters work, I was going to have to sell myself. That was the point of the thing, in fact, to market myself, go out and promote. But I was not really promoting the ideas, just myself.

I kept hearing that stupid phrase "build a brand." People were coming to me with schemes. "Get a 1-800 number, and every time someone calls it, you make money . . . "

Blah, blah, blah.

"Take that speech and get rights to it and monetize it. Put it here and here, have it pop up here, and every time you do, you get a nickel."

They went on and on.

I soon realized that this was not what I wanted to do. Not at all. It was cheap, cheesy, and just—not *fun*. I didn't want to be involved with anything like that.

To make the venture successful, I would have ultimately had to become a shameless self-promoter and build a brand on the altar of some of my most deeply held convictions. I did not feel comfortable with that and said to Yolanda, "There must be something else for me that I feel comfortable doing."

We did not abandon the nonprofit right away; we kept working hard at it. But I was not fully at peace with my actions because I did not feel that it was what I was supposed to do. We were navigating territory that was quite unknown to us and that we had to learn along the way. We had been thrown into all of this so quickly, so unexpectedly, and each step brought many new lessons. Each day found us taking things step by step and often looking back and reflecting on how we could improve and find places to make changes.

What I wanted was to take the opportunity I had and do something really solid. But not this.

Majority Matters is now dissolved.

The people I was working with were a mishmash who didn't mesh well. I folded it up a good while before I decided to run for office. I had a particularly contentious fight with a media guy to get him to shut the Facebook page down. I had to threaten legal action. The whole thing was a terrible experience.

* * *

But the period was also incredibly rewarding in other ways. I met some quite wonderful people—folks who have become friends—through the NRA. They are great. They are dedicated to a greater purpose. A lot of gun people love to talk bad about the NRA. Everyone's got a right to an opinion. But if the NRA goes away, they'll regret every bad word they said. The reason nobody is coming after *their* guns is the NRA. I can't speak publicly about the interior management troubles the NRA is experiencing now. I'm currently on the board of directors. But the NRA itself is crucial to personal freedom in this country.

I love Gun Owners of America. It is also a great organization. But there's a reason why the enemies of liberty are not attacking the Gun Owners of America with all their resources. There's a reason they have their sights set on the NRA. If they can get the NRA out of the halls of Congress, out of the House of Representatives, out of Washington, DC, you can forget gun ownership. Owning an AR-15 would be illegal in two or three years, and it might not even take that long. With the makeup we have now in the House of Representative and Senate—forget it.

The NRA has always been fantastic. They've always done right by me. Ninety-nine percent of the people in the gun community have been down-to-earth, honest people who are in this for the right reasons. Not only are they making a difference, but they are thriving because people can see how genuine they are.

We continued to travel and speak. In December of 2018, it seemed we had turned another corner. I received a call from a young man with the National Shooting Sports Foundation (NSSF). He extended an invitation for me to come to the Shooting, Hunting and Outdoor Trade (SHOT) show in Las Vegas hosted by the NSSF. This event is not open to the public but rather is for commercial buyers and sellers. Furthermore, those who wish to attend must submit an application. I was honored to have been invited, and I decided to take this gentleman up on his offer. The NSSF flew us out to Las Vegas, and we stayed for almost a week. I had the chance to speak at their political action committee (PAC) event and meet some great folks. I even met the CEO of Smith and Wesson. He graciously presented me with my favorite firearm, a Smith and Wesson Model 29 .44 magnum with a 6.5-inch barrel, aka the Dirty Harry. After I came home from the SHOT show, the wave of attention crested once again. The mailbox filled with invitations to a variety of events, requests to speak, and even interest from those on the political front. GOP groups were reaching out to me, wanting me to speak at their Lincoln-Reagan dinners. A whole host of opportunities were opening up on all fronts.

Then the most fantastic thing happened. I was at my wife's office, working with her, when the phone rang, and I answered it. On the other end was a man from the World Forum on Shooting Activities (WFSA), the sister organization of the NSSF. I was shocked when he told me that they wanted to give me an international award—the Dr. Vito Genco Ambassador Award. This award is given to someone who promotes gun rights, and this year they wanted to recognize me. I said, "Oh, okay, that's great." The man who called me was located in Connecticut. However, to attend the award ceremony, I would need to travel to Nuremberg, Germany. The WFSA would fly us over and have a hotel for us. I told him I looked forward to hearing back from him with more details and hung the phone up.

Yolanda asked, "Who was that on the phone?"

"Oh, I don't know; someone who wants to give me an award in Nuremberg, Germany," As that thought dawned on me, I repeated, "*Nuremberg, Germany!*"

The amazing thing was this: Germany was one of the places in Europe that I had always wanted to visit. Then this man called me, out of the blue, wanted me to fly to Germany, and was going to pay for the plane ticket and hotel! I couldn't believe it. Not only was I going to get to travel to Germany, but this group of people at the WFSA knew of me and wanted me there, for they had all heard my impromptu speech! The emotions were indescribable. I was finally going to travel abroad to a place I'd always wanted to visit.

So in March of 2019 we headed to Germany. Yolanda and I had a fantastic time over there for an entire week. We did a little sightseeing, and the history buff in me enjoyed being able to stand in some of the same places I had read about. But even if I had never stepped out of the hotel, just being in the country and knowing the reason why I was there was satisfying to me. I can remember looking out the window on the plane ride home and seeing the mountains in the distance. At that moment, all I could do was keep thinking to myself "I am leaving for Germany. Here I am, Mark Robinson, that little kid who used to sit on his banister pretending to fly a plane and travel the world, and now somebody called me on the phone and asked me to come to Germany. It was a surreal moment. I felt grateful and blessed that God had provided so many amazing opportunities, but this one had really taken the cake.

Once home from Germany, we continued to speak and travel. We met a lot of great people on the road, but I knew I had reached a crossroads. There was only so much talking I could do. I felt like I was back at that moment before deciding to go to the city council meeting, the moment when I realized I had to speak up. That was a crossroads moment when I told myself that sitting behind a computer and typing and making memes for social media was one thing, but the next step was to stand up and speak out. I could have been either a hypocritical keyboard warrior for life, or I could stand up and be seen, counted as one in support. I crossed that road at the city council meeting, and I now found myself at another crossroad.

18

THE DECISION

I LOVED going to church, and I loved the music in church, but I would never sing. I would not open my mouth to voice one note. I would stand still with my hymnal open and follow along, but I would not sing. Then Ms. Geraldine Dillard, the woman we called "Sarge," told me in no uncertain terms, "Two Sundays from now you are going to sing a solo."

Two Sundays later, I was standing in front of the congregation—singing a solo.

I don't know how or why, but Ms. Geraldine saw something in me that I hadn't seen and didn't want to see. Had she never reached out and forced me out of my comfort zone, I may never have discovered a talent or used it for praising my God and blessing others.

By now you perceive that this sort of thing has been a recurring theme in my life. My ninth-grade teacher recognized a knack for public speaking and helped me along the way. My high school friends, knowing I would enjoy the drill team even though I had no interest, dragged me to the first meeting.

Sometimes others see more in you than you see in yourself.

* * *

I did not go to that city council meeting thinking, "This will put my face on display, and the mayor of Greensboro can be on the lookout for me." I did not stand up to speak, thinking, "This will be just the jump start I need to break into the political scene." I did not agree to be interviewed by *Fox and Friends,* thinking, "This will be the perfect place to talk about my positions and platform." I went to that city council meeting where I spoke and then agreed to be interviewed because, ultimately, I knew it was my responsibility as a resident citizen of Greensboro and the state of North Carolina to be involved and make my voice heard.

However, almost immediately after the speech was shared on social media, the general population started making comments like, "We need this man in office" or, "I would vote for him any day."

Flattering as those words may have been at that moment, running for political office was nowhere on my agenda.

The issue of running for office surfaced again as I was interviewed on *Fox and Friends*, and again during many other interviews I gave or after events at which I spoke. After almost a year of travelling and speaking, running for office became a recurring theme of conversations I was having. But what should I do? If I ran, which position would be right for me?

I was approached by an individual suggesting that I run for North Carolina senate. At first, I thought that could be a possibility, but upon further examination, Yolanda and I decided that the senate was not right for me. We had strong, qualified people in those positions already and others who were poised to be elected who were far more suited for the job than I was. If I were going to run for political office, I wanted to be in a position best suited for my personality, someplace where I could accomplish the most good.

It was my wife who sat down with me and said, "Why don't you run for the office of lieutenant governor?"

I thought about it for a moment, sure that I could find an objection. Nope.

But surely not. We discussed it.

There was a strong conservative in that position who was on the second term of his two-term limit. So the position was about to become vacant. In our opinion, the worst thing would be for that seat of lieutenant governor to fall to a leftist. Therefore, Yolanda and I examined in depth the duties required of the position. We talked to our trusted friends and advisors, and all ultimately agreed that the office of lieutenant governor was perfectly suited for an individual like me, one who could wield power with words.

Thus, I announced my intention to run for office on July 2, 2019, while standing in front of City Hall in Greensboro. It was a hot day, and we convened at noon, but the people gathered to offer their genuine support to begin my campaign. The announcement speech in downtown Greensboro was the first true campaign speech I gave.

It was over 100 degrees that day. Many local people who followed me on Facebook were there. My friends and family were there, of course. The shirt I wore the day of the announcement never recovered. I took it to the dry cleaners, but it was ruined. I was sweating like crazy.

But that was a good day.

* * *

"Patriots, not politicians," is much more than a mere slogan to me. That's what we put on our first pieces of literature, the palm cards we passed out. I think of it more as a life motto—and a promise I intend to keep.

I am often asked what finally made me decide to run for lieutenant governor. I can't say there was one defining moment that tipped the scales in favor of running. But as I became more involved in the political landscape, I began to see the problems that existed. Between the two major parties, the Republican and Democrat, there exist extreme ideological differences. My conservative values place me squarely on the Republican side. I also believe our nation and individual states are losing sight of what the founding fathers intended our political landscape to be. Our Constitution affirms that political power and government are to come from and be given to the people, for the good of the whole. It was never intended that there would be a professional political class in this nation. Yet we have a political class whose entire identity is built around preserving themselves instead of serving the people. This is a dangerous thing for our state and nation.

From the local level, with county commissioners and mayors, to the highest level of national government with the men and women in Congress, we have individuals who have made a career out of politics. They have been in their positions for ten, twenty, or even thirty years. As a result, political stagnation occurs whenever these politicians care more about their own agendas than the concerns of the people who elected them. Then political corruption occurs when career politicians make decisions based on returning favors for patronage instead of what is best for the people as a whole. I believe this must stop. But how will it be stopped?

I entered my race for lieutenant governor without any previous political experience. I was and am an everyday, law-abiding, average citizen who has concerns for my community, state, and nation. The majority of citizens in our state and nation are just like me. We are the majority. Many citizens of North Carolina and the United States as a whole have proclaimed that I am just the type of person needed in political positions. They want someone who understands how the everyday citizen thinks and feels—someone who can put those thoughts and feelings into words that lead to action. But invariably, we hear career politicians say, "It's not that easy. There are other things to take into consideration." I have learned that "other things" often mean the complexities of political patronage. Politicians have promised to do or pay back X, Y, and Z in exchange for monetary support and votes from influential patrons.

As a side note, I believe this is why President Donald Trump was and is despised by so many career politicians in Washington. He owed them nothing, and he was working first for the American people. Washington is not the only place where these problems occur, though.

They start at the local level, continue at the state level, and culminate at the national level.

And again, how can this problem be stopped? The power belongs to average, everyday citizens. The power belongs to the people. We are the answer.

What fuels a constitutional republic? Some say liberty, freedom, or rights. But I say responsibility. Responsibility fuels a constitutional republic. And the responsibility we have as citizens is to be actively involved in what happens politically in that constitutional republic. This is one of the reasons I ran. Of course I wanted to win, but win or lose, I wanted to inspire others so they would not just be aware but become involved. Many are aware of what is happening in politics, but they are not involved. They may agree or disagree with what they see happening, but they may not fully understand enough to want to get involved.

Ask questions. Study the history and implications of decisions being made. Research the policies or bills up for discussion. Get to know your local representatives. Find out how they think and what plans for governing they have. Do the same for politicians beyond your local level. Show up for meetings and town hall gatherings. Stand up to speak if necessary. And vote. Encourage others to vote. Our vote is our final voice in the republic. Career politicians are not our masters. We the people must take our rightful place as the ones responsible for the success of the republic.

* * *

After I decided I wanted to run, the message I would be delivering came almost automatically. I had spent years on social media, putting it out there, honing it, learning how to say it the best way I could. It was the same thing that built up those 15,000 followers before that speech. It was the same thing that came out during that speech. And it was the same things that came after that speech when I continued to talk about on social media platforms and platforms beyond. This message has five core values.

- Pro-life

- Pro-Constitution (including the Second Amendment)

- Standing up for true education, parents' rights, school choice, and against left-wing indoctrination in education

- Standing up for our military veterans

- Standing up for law enforcement

If you go back and look at my social media pages, those are the things I talk about most of the time. There's a smattering of social issues in there as well, but they are often connected to and driven by those values and key interests.

I threw the gauntlet down when I announced. I was pretty popular then, and a lot of people had been urging me to run. When I announced I was running for lieutenant governor, people were excited.

Platforms are built on the foundation of beliefs, and beliefs are often shaped by experiences. I am blessed to have a foundation laid on faith in the almighty God. I am blessed to have been raised with biblical morals and values. I am blessed to have experienced a particular set of circumstances with which many in the political landscape are not acquainted.

While there are many important issues to be addressed, those five areas became my focus. First, I want to see that our state and national constitutions are upheld by recognizing that we govern by and for the people. The Constitution and the Bill of Rights are the fortress of our freedom, the fortress that protects our rights and liberties. But a fortress with no firepower is useless.

The Second Amendment is the firepower of our Constitution.

One of the times I am distressed is when elected officials say they support the Second Amendment because they support hunting. But the amendment has nothing to do with hunting or sport. The Second Amendment was intentionally put into our Constitution to protect the people should the government become tyrannical.

If the government decides to become ruler of the people instead of the people's servant, the Second Amendment allows the people to stand against the government and remind it that the people are in charge. Many have forgotten that when people lose their ability to defend themselves, governments will inevitably become tyrannical. It is not even a question of maybe. Throughout the twentieth century, we've seen example after example of governments that became tyrannical and terrorized the people they were supposed to be serving. In every case, their tyranny started with disarmament and ended in misery, despair, and often, mass death.

I was once challenged by someone who said, "Well, the United Kingdom has gun control, and they aren't tyrannical."

I reminded them of the story of a family whose child was very sick. Due to socialized medicine, they were unable to get the child properly treated in their own country. When they decided to go see a specialist in another country, their government told them they could not go. They had to stay at home and watch their child die, untreated. If that is not a tyrannical government, forcing parents to stay home instead of taking their child to be treated, then I don't know what is. When it comes to tyranny, most think of Adolf Hitler or Joseph Stalin, but not many consider the tyranny of the career politicians who live the high life in the capital while the streets of their home districts are lined with human waste, the homeless, and drug addicts. These politicians were elected to work for the people to create positive change. However, they treat their voters as pawns who are ripped off and cast off once they make it in office.

I find that many Americans seem to have the false impression that our government will never become too big nor step too far out of line. They can't imagine a situation that would cause American citizens to need to take up arms. However, there are government officials across this nation destroying cities with policies and socialist agendas that were never intended to occur under our Constitution. The more this continues, the more resistance we will see from the people until it reaches a boiling point. Then this will be the question: Can the American people defend themselves from a corrupt, tyrannical government? This is one of the reasons I am passionate about the integrity of our Constitution, especially the Second Amendment.

Protecting the lives of the unborn is the most pressing social issue of our time. I am the ninth of ten children. If my mother were pregnant with me today, she surely would be told to abort me if she sought advice from an abortionist or pro-choice individual. Let's consider the current rhetoric heard on a daily basis: a woman living in poverty who already has other children to feed should spare another child from having to grow up impoverished; a child should be spared from living in a less than desirable home with an abusive, alcoholic father; abortion is a kindness to children who would be born into families unable to provide every possible opportunity.

Abortion advocates speak as if killing unborn children is an altruistic act. Today's abortion providers would assure my mother that aborting me would be her best option to avoid a life full of pain for herself and for what would be her child. If she asked anything about what pain I might feel in the womb, she would be assured that I was nothing more than a clump of cells, a mass of tissue, not a living soul with an alert mind and feelings.

Had I been aborted, I would have missed out on all the great things God had planned for me. Sure, I would not have endured the trials and hard times, but those were a part of the way God chose to make me the man I am now. God guided me through those bad times for a reason, for he had a plan for my life. Abortion does not save a child from future hardship; it destroys a child's future potential.

Last year, around the world, approximately 42 million children were aborted in the womb, which means that 42 million potential humans were never given the chance to be realized. Somewhere among those 42 million may have been someone God would bless with the intellect and knowledge to cure cancer. But the potential of that child was discarded like trash, never even given a fighting chance. I ask myself: How many times has this been justified since *Roe v. Wade*? Americans claim to uphold life, liberty, and justice. Many claim that *Roe v. Wade* is about life, liberty, and justice. Yet under the umbrella of legality, millions of lives are thrown away every year. Those lives never had the chance to experience liberty. Those lives never received justice from mankind. And most sadly, those lives were not even acknowledged as living.

Just as we brought an end to slavery for the causes of liberty and justice, we must end abortion for the cause of life. We must acknowledge that calling something "legal" does not make it just or right. We must acknowledge that life exists from the moment of conception. God endows his creation with life, and each individual has the God-given right to life. That is why I am so determined to fight for the unborn.

My goal is to tackle and improve issues concerning education by making changes in the classroom, not by blindly throwing more money at the issues. Ultimately, I want to see that the classroom becomes a place where parents, children, and teachers experience success. We must create a culture of success that starts with our elementary schools and grows with our children. However, there are a number of obstacles in the way of creating that culture of success.

One of those obstacles is a lack of strong, structured discipline within our schools. And by discipline in the school, I do not mean that the teacher must take on the responsibility of teaching the children right from wrong. That is the exclusive responsibility of parents or guardians.

What we need in our schools is a strong set of rules to deter and prevent behaviors that hinder learning and endanger students or staff. The standard must be firm from day one: a standard that says, "When you walk through these doors you will not bully, you will not fight, you will not attack your teacher, and you will not deal or use drugs." We need zero tolerance. A child who cannot meet the school's behavioral expectations should not be allowed to undermine the success of the other students. The education system is meant to be a safe place for children to learn. If a child is hindering their own and others' learning by misbehaving, the child must be stopped or removed from the classroom until they can demonstrate proper behavior. Ideally, these children would be returned to their parents or guardians until they are able to behave at school.

Although I realize there are a host of factors to consider, we need to be serious about having a firm standard and upholding that standard from day one. Students must know that when they come to school, they will be nurtured and protected. They must also know that when they do not follow the standard for behavior, there will be strict consequences. Parents and guardians must know this as well and must be ready to accept the consequences when their children refuse to adhere to the rules and guidelines of the school. Teachers also ought to feel safe in school. Many teachers experience horrendous treatment at the hands of students and feel helpless because the administration refuses to deal properly with incorrigible students. Our teachers must know they are supported by those of us who represent them in our government. We have to help our schools establish and enforce firm standards of behavior and systems of discipline that foster a safe learning environment. The success of our schools and students depends on the success of our teachers.

Beyond behavior and discipline issues, we have to tackle the issue of social engineering that is taking place in our education system. I have heard stories of students being directed to watch CNN, or PBS, or— Lord, help us—MSNBC, organizations that are clearly biased in their reporting, and then asked to write a report on what they learned. This is just one of the ways that our students are not being taught how to think, but rather *what* to think. I have an example that is even closer to my own experience. Recently, a teacher told a student that she couldn't submit a Black History Month report on the first lieutenant governor in North Carolina history—in other words, *me*—because the teacher did not believe I was a good example. The teacher suggested that the student write about the rapper Tupac Shakur instead.

That's indoctrination. And it was most likely because she didn't like my politics or because she doesn't like me.

As one who loves history, I believe teachers should be taught and allowed to present all sides of our history and allow students to wrestle with and decide where they stand on the issues. Additionally, our children and teens are being indoctrinated with principles derived from socialist dogma. That, combined with the fact that students often learn a distorted version of history, has produced a generation who do not understand the dangers of socialism. We have a generation of students who have been taught the principles of socialism—on paper. However, we have neglected to teach them the failures of socialism in the real world. They are not being taught the lessons learned when prosperous countries fell to ruin after socialist governments took control. We must change the way our children are taught.

I am now on the North Carolina Board of Education, where I advocate for changes to the curriculum in our state to ensure that our students are taught the basics and are given a solid foundation from the earliest levels. I believe we must begin at the elementary level and move through the education system to middle and high schools. We must order our steps as we do so. Teachers and parents alike have long expressed their frustration with what and how our students are taught. It is past time that we take back the reins of education and guide our state by the standards and principles that work best for North Carolina's children.

That starts with an intense concentration on what is sometimes called the three "Rs" of education for grades one through six. Those three "Rs" are reading, writing, and arithmetic. These subjects provide the solid foundation students need to be successful in all other areas of education. As it stands now, we have students who somehow make it through our educational system without being proficient in these basic areas. In North Carolina, the proficiency of elementary and middle school students in 2021 to read at the appropriate grade level is 45.6 percent. In my home county of Guilford, it is 43.5 percent. And at Allen Middle School, it is 30.7 percent. Almost 70 percent of children there cannot read at even a minimum proficiency. More than half of North Carolina students are reading below their grade level. By the way, the 2021 grade level proficiency for math at Allen Middle School was 14.8

WE ARE THE MAJORITY!

percent.[1] The educational establishment should feel great shame over this. Beyond that, we have young people in the workforce today, even in management positions, who may be able to operate a computer but cannot write a coherent paragraph. We must change this, and we must begin this process at the elementary level.

I'm vitally concerned in getting health care benefits up to snuff for North Carolina veterans. North Carolina has a rich history of military service, dating back to the earliest days of our revolution. Additionally, our state is home to three of the largest military installations in the country. Our rich history, our current service, and the valiant service of now retired or wounded soldiers in our state make it a necessity for our elected officials to create a system of veteran care that is the gold standard in this nation.

The process starts by no longer taxing our veterans' pensions, especially those of our most grievously wounded and ill veterans. They should have quick, easy access to the care they need. This is just the beginning of the long list of benefits we need to offer our veterans in North Carolina.

Law enforcement officers are another group of public servants who need our support, and they were the final area of focus in my platform. Everyone who has watched the news over the past decade has heard the false narratives being pushed by leftists and their social justice warrior allies. Florida, Baltimore, and Missouri have all experienced the effects of high-profile cases in which false cries of racism and police brutality have been used to defend the actions of criminals. When faced with these false narratives, many of our elected officials cower and choose political correctness over law and order. In short, they throw our police officers under the bus.

Elected officials need to stand beside our officers and have the courage to expose the media's lies and the false narratives of the social justice warriors. Police officers across the country are being ridiculed,

---

1   https://ncreports.ondemand.sas.com/src/school?school=410316&year=2021&lng=en

harassed, assaulted, and in some cases assassinated. This is a direct result of criminals being emboldened when officials choose to side with the criminals instead of the police officers.

This also leads to our law enforcement becoming reactive in fighting crime, instead of proactive. Many officers today feel handcuffed. When facing a choice between confronting suspects or staying in their patrol cars, many are choosing to do the latter. These officers understand that in today's climate, not only is it difficult to deal with these suspects in dangerous situations, but it is also difficult to deal with the elected officials in the halls of government.

We need people in office who will support and empower the police, not the criminals. Law enforcement stands as a thin blue line between chaos and stability. Elected officials must ensure that line remains strong and firm—not unregulated, but strong and firm. Every day, these officers put their lives on the line for us. We have to stand up for them as if our own lives depended on them, because sometimes, they literally do.

19

THE PRIMARY TRAIL

AFTER YOLANDA SAID, "Why not lieutenant governor?" I thought about it for quite a while.

Then I decided, yes, I'm going to do that. I'm going to do what I've always said for years that a candidate should be doing. I'm going to go Bulworth and stay Bulworth. I'm going to get up on stage and tell it like it is. And the news media is going to call me names, and I will make some good points, and that will probably be the end of it. But I'm going to see if what I believe is right and if people agree that what I believe is right.

We went about the process of finding a campaign consultant. It wasn't a sophisticated quest, by any means. We went on the internet and did a search for "conservative political consultants, North Carolina." I called the top choice. They never called me back. The second one told me how much they would cost, which was an incredible amount for us. They didn't even ask me who I was or my history.

Then I called the third one, Conservative Connections, headed by Conrad Pogorzelski III.

I got Conrad right away. He said, "Yeah, I know who you are. Let's meet and talk."

We met at a Panera Bread restaurant in Greensboro. Conrad is a young man. He looks as if he is barely out of high school, much less college. I told myself, "Appearances can be deceiving. Let me listen to what this young man has to say."

It was one of the best decisions I've made in my life.

We sat down. Conrad asked me to tell him my story. He was the one who did the listening! I told him about myself and how I feel about things politically. I may not have recognized it at the time, but the mental gears of this remarkable young man were grinding away.

He said, "This is great. We can do this."

And we started from there. He didn't ask for any money. He told me we could raise money. We just started right there. We crafted our message and started campaigning.

* * *

I had my message together, and I started drilling that in. I needed to get that message out there, so my campaign speeches at the beginning were virtually all the same. The length and content of each speech depended on where I was and how much time I had, but no matter how much time I had or where it was, I covered those five points.

A lot of people today think I wrote that speech at the Greensboro City Council Meeting. I didn't. I don't write speeches now. I tell my people I'm about to "go Bulworth," and tell the truth. That movie is hilarious. That church scene? I could watch that over and over again.

When I first started to do public speaking, I began making notes, like bullet points, and following them. After a while, my wife told me to stop doing that because I didn't look genuine. So I stopped. I realized that I don't need that. For lack of a better way of saying it, all those points and examples are just floating around in my head, and all I have to do is open my mouth and let it come out. And somehow it comes out in an organized fashion.

I don't write down anything, but I do spend a great deal of time thinking about what I might say. The general theme will depend on the situation, but often I don't plan anything. For instance, I have to give a speech at the North Carolina Republican Convention soon. I probably won't give much thought to what I have to say. It's a convention, and it's Republicans. I'm not talking about taxes. I'm not talking about the amount of money we're going to spend on education. Instead, it's about values we share, values this country needs. I'm rallying the troops at a Republican convention. I don't need notes for that. I can speak directly from my heart.

So I began to extemporize on my five points. If I had thirty minutes at a women's group, I would hit all those topics evenly. But if I were in a gun store, I would touch on all those topics but spend most of my time emphasizing my thoughts on the Second Amendment. But I always try to connect that with the other points. In a gun store, I might make a shift like this: "Now, we're in a gun store. Why do y'all care about education, especially if you have young ones at school? Why do some people say the Second Amendment should be ignored or nullified in our Constitution? It goes back to lack of education, to people not understanding how our Constitution came to be, why the Second Amendment is part of the Bill of Rights. Most of all, why it is so vital for us to have that right? It all points back to education."

Making such transitions was a way to get my five-point message across.

Or take my pro-life message. God gives you your life, and he gives you a right to your life. And after he gives you your life, he gives you the responsibility to defend your life and the lives of those you love. I would cross over and make connections to my other points, trying to shape it to the audience.

My emphasis on veterans? Bringing that in is easy, especially in military-base-rich North Carolina. People don't respect veterans, don't take care of them as they should, because we don't know the history of the wars that have been fought, the military history of our country. Vietnam, Korea, World War II, World War I—we have often forgotten about those things because our educational system is no longer teaching us about them.

Then, of course, it's easy to make the connection between veterans and law enforcement. Veterans put their lives on the line when they are defending and preparing to fight for us, and policemen do the same here at home.

That message resonated with many people in North Carolina. There was enough substance there that people could disagree with me in some areas, yet still want to vote for me because I spoke about something that was very important to them. Everybody's not going to agree with everything you say, but I do believe the message we had resonated with most people.

* * *

Some people who disagreed with me on abortion were all in on the Second Amendment. There were some who disagreed on parts of my Second Amendment views but were all in on supporting law enforcement. People who disagreed on some parts of law enforcement were all in on supporting the Second Amendment. There were those who only cared about education but were all in there. And there were many who loved all five points. It was a strong coalition. I didn't know it at the time, but it had the makings of a winning coalition. We had enough meat on the bone of our message to establish a lot of support right off the bat.

I had support from the local Republican political community from the beginning. Sixth District chairman Lee Hayward and Congressman Mark Walker were very excited about my decision to run.

Conrad stayed in Gaston County. Sometimes Conrad would come to my house, and we'd work from there. Sometimes I'd go to his office. Conrad's youthful appearance leads many to underestimate him. I'm very glad I didn't make that mistake. He is extremely plugged in and knows everyone, particularly around Gaston County. He really was a master at Conservative Connections.

I also had the advantage of spending the year before I ran, making many public speeches following the Greensboro City Council speech. I was speaking at events everywhere. I spoke at my local party meetings. I spoke at Lincoln-Reagan dinners, the principal Republican grassroots fundraising events, across the state. I was getting known for my speaking and my message *before* I started to run. I was delivering the message to local GOP meetings before I was running for office.

And time and again, people at these events urged me to run for office because they loved the message I delivered. This was a constant refrain. When I announced my candidacy for lieutenant governor, those people across the state were very excited. I had a built-in base of engaged supporters immediately. This gave me a distinct advantage over my opponents in the race.

Now sometimes I get asked about why I am not just strongly conservative but am also very outspoken about being a Republican. Here's the reason: I learned the *truth* about Republicans. The lie about Republicans is that Republicans are a bunch of old rich white men who care only about old rich white men and love only rich people. That is a big lie. One of the Republican Party's founding principles was to stand up for the lowest of the low in society.

Can the *New York Times* dispute it? Can William Barbour dispute it? Can Nancy Pelosi dispute it? No. They can't dispute it because it's true. The Republican Party was formed for standing up for the constitutional republic and for ending the institution of slavery. Members of the Republican Party fought and prosecuted the Civil War to pull this nation together after Democrats had torn it apart expressly because Democrats did not want a system in this country that allowed black people to be anything but second-class citizens or slaves. The Republican Party was formed to make sure that did not continue to exist. After slavery ended and later when Jim Crow was instituted in the South, the Republican Party continued to fight for freedom and equality for black people. They fought to give women the right to vote. They did everything they could to repudiate Jim Crow. Today we as a party stand for the same principles we stood for back then. Nothing has changed.

People can't argue with this. It's the truth. It's not some lie I made up because I like Ronald Reagan or Donald Trump. It's the truth, and I don't apologize for being Republican. I'm proud of it! If you think I'm wrong, prove me wrong. Show me in history where the Democratic Party ever did any pure and good for black folks. They put us in slave shacks and then housing projects and the ghetto. The Democratic Party is the party of welfare checks and dependency. The Republican Party is the party of freedom and opportunity.

* * *

After I announced, we started campaigning. We set up the campaign website. We set up a financial entity to raise money. I went downtown to file all the papers with the county and state. We had to pay the $1,367 fee on filing day. That made me an official candidate. We ramped up our efforts even more after that. By ramped up, I mean we had to do a great deal of fundraising at first. I was a first-time candidate, with zero political experience. Because I already had some recognition, I could skip over creating general name recognition and concentrate on getting better known and raising the money we needed to start rolling.

Conrad's firm had a staff, and that was the entirety of my campaign staff at that point. Raising money was tough, which was hard to do at first. There were a couple of months when I didn't think we would be able to pay our invoice from Conrad—and he didn't charge that much for what he did compared to some! But every month, we made it. No funds ever had to come out of pocket to pay him. We always made it.

The further in we got, the more we got our message out there, and the more people embraced us. We started attending a series of forums where all the Republican candidates for lieutenant governor would be on stage and take questions. I had a lot of suggestions from Conrad about how to handle those things, but I also had my own experience. We did well. Whenever I left those forums, those other candidates knew they were in trouble. We walked out of every one of those debates and meetings feeling victorious. When we left, the people in the halls knew we were the front runners.

Nevertheless, several people in that primary race still didn't take me seriously. There were some who had held office, who had plenty of money. They looked at me and, I hate to say it, thought they were smarter than I was. They thought that on the right stage, at the right moment, they would be able to supplant me with their superior intellect and knowledge. They were confident of that.

There was one particular forum in Charlotte where several of the candidates were lined up, there was an audience, and we were taking questions from them. Pat McCory, the former governor, was the moderator. I walked in and looked around this opulent place. The guy had a private chef. It was really something. I felt like this was the moment that some of these candidates thought they might make their move, show themselves to be the savviest, and get ahead with these influential Republicans.

That didn't happen.

I believe it was at that meeting when the other candidates truly knew they were in trouble. We were articulate, passionate, informed. We ruled the roost. We took over that room from the beginning and didn't relinquish it. This was primarily because we had the right message at the right time, and we knew how to get it out there. That became obvious to everyone there.

It was not just me making a speech. It was a combination of things Conrad had prepared me for and the strategy we had worked out. We went in with a plan about how we should answer the questions we thought we could get. We went over contingency answers if things came up that we didn't expect. We had done enough events to know what was coming. And we did our homework.

For example, they asked me about the minimum wage. "What do you think about raising the minimum wage to fifteen dollars an hour?" The others made standard answers, and frankly some of them were incoherent.

I answered, "I'm against raising the minimum wage. I agree with the other candidates here that it will hurt business. But here is why I'm really against raising the minimum wage: as an elected official, I don't believe it's my job to be worried about this. When I look at the people of North Carolina, I don't see 'minimum people.' I don't see minimum talent. I don't see minimum opportunity. I see people who can maximize their opportunities, people who have maximum potential and maximum talent. It's my job to make sure we build an economy where we have jobs that are not all minimum wage jobs, but jobs that allow them to maximize their talent and possibilities. Minimum wage is an afterthought for me. That's something for high school kids. If you're talking about adults, you're talking about building a life. We have to build an economy where that's going to happen. We need to help create jobs that pay three, four, or five times whatever the minimum wage is. It's also my job as an elected official to make sure we have an educational system and a training system so we have people ready to take those jobs when they arrive."

The people in that room went crazy with applause when they heard that. They hadn't gotten an answer like that before, not from any politician—federal, state, or local—in living memory, that's for sure. They had never heard the concept. Of course, Conrad and I had planned for this. We knew at some point the minimum wage question was going to come up, and I already had worked out that response. Those are my true feelings about it, of course, but I'd thought it through and was prepared. The good thing about having Conrad around was that I could bounce my responses and ideas off him before taking them out, and he might say, "Oh, that's fantastic." But then he'd tell me that I ought to add in this, this, and this—tweak it this way. So we honed the message.

Our campaign turned the corner that night. We frightened our competition because after that night, some of those guys began campaigns of lies and whispers aimed at me. They lied and said I had a dishonorable discharge from the military, that I was in financial trouble, not just in the past, but at that moment. What blew me away was that I have my DD2-14, which states I have an honorable discharge from the Army. I got a VA loan on my house. And I'd already been telling people on the road that I'd filed for bankruptcy before I even started running for office. It was part of my story. So either they spread lies or talked about things that were well known as if they were bombshells.

I thought, "Guys, if you want to tell somebody something new, you're going to have to go all the way back to high school and find out how I was almost run over by a train."

Now *that* was a secret for a long time because I didn't want my mamma to ever find out about it!

I was running against eight others. My top opponent in the race was State Senator Andy Wells. He had funding, and he was already in office. Then there was a former congresswoman named Renee Ellmers. There was a former state representative named Scott Stone out of Mecklenburg County. There was Deborah Cochran, who used to be the mayor of Mount Airy. She was also a schoolteacher. There was a fellow from New Bern, a former semi-pro baseball player and restaurant owner, Buddy Bengel. There was John Ritter, an attorney from Moore County. There was Greg Gebhardt, a National Guardsman. And there was Mark Johnson, the superintendent of education of North Carolina at the time. We were worried about people getting his name and my name confused. That happens more often than you might think.

Republicans are notorious for putting up candidates who are "the next in line for the job." I think this has cost us more elections than almost anything. That said, why did I not run for the state assembly or mayor of Greensboro? Two reasons. I don't think I have the right temperament. I particularly don't think I'd be suited to be mayor of Greensboro, given the situation of the city council. It would have been an ongoing, contentious relationship with a bunch of left-wing nutcases until some other people could run and replace them. There are other people better suited for that task.

The lieutenant governor's office has duties that must be fulfilled, yes, but it also offers an outlet to stand up and speak out for the things I believe in and provides the amount of freedom I need to do that, while at the same time allowing me to learn the inner workings of government and giving me a good place to learn those things.

The second reason I decided to do it was to prove to people that it could be done, that a normal private citizen could run for that office. Even if we didn't win, I would have shown that I could make a good run and talk about some things that mattered. That's what I thought would happen. I would make a good run, and if I didn't win, so be it. I'd have shown people that an ordinary citizen can actually do it.

Then the more I got into it, the more elected officials I met, the more I thought, *Hey, if that guy can do it, I surely can. If he can hold office for thirty years, I can hold it for four.* It dawned on us that we really could win and do what I wanted to do, which was to send a message to status quo politicians that the ordinary citizens of this state can win. And I wanted to send a message to the people of the state that they, too, can run, and they very well might win if they run the right way and have the right kind of message.

To a large extent, this worked. I meet people who tell me that because of me, they have decided to run for city council, or school board, or whatever it may be.

When the primary was over and I won, I heard from Deborah Cochran. I heard from Mark Johnson. I heard from Greg Gephardt. John Ritter later told me he would have called but didn't have the number. That was it. Renee Ellmers and I have had a good conversation. But there were others who later were in the same room with me and refused to approach me. It was sometimes acrimonious.

But that is a minor matter. My motivation was the message, along with my conviction that if I was spending this time away from my family, from my home—I was not going to do this and lose, especially without giving it my all. So I gave it my all, every day. And I drew energy and hope from the people I was speaking to and talking with. They loved what I was saying. They were so happy someone was talking about putting their own beliefs and convictions into action. I heard it again and again. That is energizing! It helped me to remember what I was doing it for—not merely to win the lieutenant governor's seat, but to get to a place where I could do something about the plethora of bad decisions and bad policies I saw being enacted and enforced, to do the right thing instead. And that's what took me through making the fourth or fifth speech of the day. It still does.

At some points, I was not having fun, I have to say. It was duty that kept me going. We did an infamous 100-county tour. We toured all 100 counties in North Carolina in the span of a month and a half or so, and it was exhausting. Well, we got to 99 of 100 counties, and we made up for that by going to Guilford County twice. I had to cancel on Pasquotank County and go to Guilford County for a forum there; otherwise, we spoke in every county. I was going to skip the Guilford Forum because it was my home turf, but my county GOP chairman called me and told me there were some ladies who were absolutely counting on my being there, so I had to do that. There were times when I was giving five speeches in a day, traveling to four and five counties a day. That was rough. Conrad and his people, of course, did the massive behind-the-scenes organization.

* * *

How was I getting paid during all this? God kind of lined everything up for this run. I left my job at Davis Furniture on August 17, 2018. My wife had started her nonprofit shortly before that, and it took off. In 2016, she had her first meeting where all her providers came together. It filled a small library's conference room. The next year, she had to have it at a hotel conference center, and there was a massive group of people. So by the time I was ready to run for office, Yolanda's nonprofit was providing a salary for her that was enough to support us. After I left Davis, I either was making speeches or was downtown at my wife's office, helping her with her work. This is something my son does now. When I ran for office, I stopped doing that, and that's when my son started filling in. Now my son does it full-time.

One thing that made it easier on Yolanda in 2020 was that when COVID-19 hit, she didn't have to go out and do in-person visits for a while. This made it easier for her to do her job at the time and participate to an extent in the campaign with me. That's come to an end now, and she has to hit the road again and, more importantly, train others she's hired to do visits and to administer the paperwork, which is an immense job in itself. But Yolanda was making enough to pay our bills in 2020 so I could run for lieutenant governor.

Of course, when I won, I started getting a paycheck! Now my funds pay most of the bills. I'm not really sure what she does with the money she earns—probably something smart. Anyway, that's how we survived. It was a blessing.

We won the primary in March 2020. Most political people around me expected that there was going to be a runoff between me and Andy Wells. Conrad was convinced there would be a runoff. But my wife said, "There will be no runoff."

Yolanda was right. We got 31.3 percent of the vote. We won straight out and didn't have a runoff.

But the biggest shock awaited us. It came from the Democratic primary.

20

THE GENERAL

I HAD BEEN SURE I would be taking on a lady named Terry Van Duyn as the Democratic Party nominee for lieutenant governor. She was a white woman out of Mecklenburg County who was very, *very* liberal. I was greatly looking forward to slamming her on her crazy positions. I wasn't going to hold back at all. I was going to attack like a lion. I had material lined up to use, and I was ready to jump into the fray. Terry Van Duyn represented everything I was against in politics, and I thought her personal style was condescending and patronizing to the very people she wanted to represent. I was going to accuse her of being a racist, and I would have loved to have done so because I believe it is true. I love to accuse these left-wingers of being racists for two reasons. First, because I am certain that they are. But second? They hate it. Oh, do they hate it. It leaves them sputtering in rage. It's the worst thing you can say to them. I was ready to come at her like a rhetorical sledgehammer. I would have egged her on in order to get her to attack me in return. I was looking forward to responding and, frankly, getting into it.

But—Terry Van Duyn didn't win.

All those plans became beside the point. Another person won, State Representative Yvonne Holley, and Van Duyn conceded the race so the Democrats could avoid a runoff. Holley was an older black lady. We were shocked. We had not expected this. We had to reconsider our strategery. Because she was an older black female, it would not look good for me to attack her. She very much reminded me of a very proper lady I might encounter at St. Stephen Church. I had to be careful on stage with her and watch the things I said about her positions. I did not want to appear to bully her in any way. It's not like Holley was some weak old lady, of course. She was certainly not feeble-minded at all.

We were still confident we would win. We had by far the superior message. It was one of those times in life when you're waiting for the other shoe to drop, for something to go wrong. Well it did.

Everything in the campaign was going great until we found out that Michael Bloomberg had dumped eight million dollars into the race for Holley with about a month to go before the general election. We felt like we were in trouble. I told my wife, "Well, if this is what buries us, then so be it."

I was already making plans about what I would do if I lost that race.

My wife kept assuring me that we weren't going to lose, that we were going to win.

Right.

Eight million dollars.

We did have some hope because we thought the Bloomberg money might not have enough time to make a big difference for Holley. It *did* make a difference. But they made a strategic mistake of enormous proportions. It was hard to believe they could be that stupid. But Democrats are ideologues or in the pocket of special interests for the most part and are seldom in touch with regular people's concerns. The Holley campaign used the money for mailers and radio and television ads to hammer me on, of all things, climate change.

Climate change, in a race for lieutenant governor of North Carolina. They used a clip from one of the debates where I said that when

WE ARE THE MAJORITY!

administering the energy needs of the people of North Carolina, I would rely on science—"and by science, I don't mean the junk science of global warming and climate change." They jumped all over that, saying "Mark Robinson thinks global warming is junk science."

Guess what? Most of the people of North Carolina *know* global warming is junk science. I thought for sure what they would attack me on was some of my old Facebook posts that were so inflammatory. But no, nothing on guns. Nothing on my opinion of Michelle Obama. Not even any sly ways of calling me an Uncle Tom. It was my views on global warming they went after.

This was a gift. We didn't even try to answer. There was no need. We just continued with our message and paid very little attention to her. We didn't use her name in our advertising. We kept to our message.

We didn't have much money for television. We did some television advertising with the Republican candidate for governor, Dan Forest, and some very limited advertising on cable in the state, particularly during some A&E crime shows, the History Channel, and Spectrum, the cable provider that also does public affairs programing.

Instead of being television-based, we ran our campaign on social media. I had a video on social media that I filmed on my back porch for free where I described my childhood and talked about my beliefs. That video to date has about three million views. We had some other advertisements we made while I was standing in my living room or down at the campaign office. We did it all with cellphones, small handheld cameras, and green screens. These were wildly successful. We got hundreds of thousands of views and shares.

By October 29, 2020, the polls were looking okay. I was at forty-seven percent. Holley was at forty-four percent, with nine percent undecided.[1] But a three percent gap is not unbridgeable by any means, and the campaign was far from over. Those nine percent undecideds were

---

1   https://wwwcache.wral.com/asset/news/state/nccapitol/2020/10/29/19360710/PollPrint-DMID1-5oon3xggr.pdf

made up disproportionately of young moderate women and Latinos—not a traditional Republican stronghold![2]

Conrad's people are as young as he is, and they are all focused on social media. I was already very comfortable using it and using it well, of course. And that's basically how we ran our whole campaign. We had a shoestring budget, but everything we did was very effective. And one thing that really helped us was that during the primary, we had done that 100-county tour and had been all around the state. People didn't just know who I was, they had *seen* me in person, met me, and shook my hand. By the time COVID-19 shut everything down for a while, we had already gotten out there. COVID-19 hit and we went into lockdown, then when things opened back up, we did as much as we could where we could, but it was difficult to operate with the restrictions.

Meanwhile, Yvonne Holley's message was all over the place, politically speaking. Her people did not use social media effectively for her. Her campaign seemed like a muddle. If somebody asked her what her message was, it might have been something like, "Don't vote for the Republican."

* * *

How does political fundraising happen? Phone calls. That's the worst part of this whole process. From the get-go, Conrad would contact me every day and say, "Did you make any phone calls?" I would say, "Sure, I made a few." I have to admit that I was very resistant to the process of making phone calls. At that point, I was cold-calling people. "Hello, I'm Mark Robinson, and I'm running for lieutenant governor . . . " I sometimes spent three and four hours a day doing this. At first, I was trying to do it alone, then I had a young man, John Harris, sit with me, and we'd make calls off a list that Conrad put together. These were Republican donors.

During the primary, it was very difficult to raise money. There

---

2   https://www.wral.com/poll-cooper-maintains-wide-lead-over-forest/19360496/

were nine candidates. Most of our money was raised online through an app called Nation Building. I had very few people who maxed out on my campaign in the primary. Most of my donations were from small donors. That's why in the last stages of the primary, we didn't have the money to do what we wanted to do with advertising, and my campaign manager told me we had to do our 100-county tour. So we hit the road. And while we were out there on the road, we were raising money. That was much easier for me.

That 100-county tour really made the difference in both the primary and the general election.

When we won the primary, it was big news. It was big news because I won over eight other candidates without a runoff. It was also big news because the election was now between a black man and a black woman. In either case, the winner would be the first black lieutenant governor of North Carolina. So this made the news and got our names out there. I was speaking and appearing on this show and that show, and I developed a lot more name recognition.

That made raising money during the general election much easier.

I would call people on the phone and say, "My name is Mark Robinson . . ."

They would answer, "Yeah, I know who you are." And they would have heard about my positions, and they would tell *me* what they thought and which of my positions they agreed with or had some issue with.

It was much better. They would ask why I was calling, and I would tell them straight out that it was a fundraising call. They were usually happy to be asked, and I would hear things I'd never heard before, such as, "Yes, I'll give you five hundred dollars. I believe in what you're saying." Or "Let me talk to my wife and see if we can max out the donation."

And they would write a check to the campaign for several thousand dollars. This happened quite a bit. There was great value in making the phone calls then, and I did it. That's how it happens. Campaign funds are raised deliberately. And in order for the effort to be effective, it has got to be done by the candidate.

Now if you're Donald Trump, you might not have to do this. You can make a recording. Donald Trump can spend his personal time going after big whale donors. But for a candidate on the local or state level, you are going to have to be involved in the process. The only way to avoid this is to be rich or extremely famous. I am neither. If you are a new guy just getting started, you have to call them on the phone and make that connection. That's what I had to do.

There were days during the primary when I didn't make a nickel. But there was never a day in the general when I didn't raise something. And some days, I would sit in my office making calls, and within two or three hours, I'd raise $30,000. It continues to be very effective. I call donors now, and they're excited. They know who I am. They know what I stand for.

This second stage—it's not a big secret that I am exploring running for governor—is going to be a lot of that, going through lists. A good list is political gold. For political consultants, lists are commodities they trade. They beg for other people's list of donors. They make deals to get their lists.

The night of the primary, we were at a barn-like meeting place that had been built for square dancing out near High Point. We had quite a few people there. It was a very nervous night. I was pacing the floor; it was not like anything I've ever been through in my life. I felt like so much was riding on this. We went ahead in the voting and stayed ahead. Our lead continued to build and build. At one point during the night, Conrad had been looking at this and that, checking on counties that had come in. Then he started tallying things up on a piece of paper, peering at the screen, and writing more. He got down to the bottom of the piece of paper and drew a line under it, added it all up, and circled that number.

"It's over," he said.

"Are you serious?" I asked.

"Nobody else has a pathway. No one has a way they can beat you."

Sure enough, about ten minutes after that one of my opponents called and conceded. That was it. Jubilation. Congratulations. I went up on stage and gave a speech. There was a little media there, but not much. I told everybody it was now on to the general election.

The news media at that point figured that I was an anomaly. A reporter at WXII had been following me since the city council speech. I don't mean this as an insult, but I think he was very skeptical about me, very skeptical about grassroots conservatism in general, and said so. When I was doing Majority Matters, he ran a story about that and tried to question some of the paperwork he claimed was improperly filed. This wasn't true; all our paperwork was in order.

When we ran in the primary, he interviewed me. He said he was very shocked that I had won. He thought I didn't have a chance. I'm sure he was waiting at some point to find a "gotcha," to say, "I told you, this guy is nobody." I'm not sure how he could believe a black Republican would not have a very good chance at winning state office in North Carolina. It's a 50-50 state with a large black population, of which I am one.

But that's the way many reporters are. They are very out of touch. They live in their own world of left-wing nuttiness, conspiracies, and silly beliefs about those whose politics they disagree with. Many are completely out of touch with reality.

The primary was before the COVID-19 lockdown. Right after we won that, the lockdown came. The general election was muddled up by the lockdown. We slowly started to get back out and go to events late in the summer. We were demonized by people in the media. Dan Forest was getting hammered over that issue. My wife in particular got COVID-19, and I'm pretty sure I had it too. We had to quarantine for a couple of weeks. For her, it was coughing and fever for a time. I didn't feel it much, but I did have that peculiar experience of losing my taste and smell. But we got over it and got back on track.

Then in the fall, we had debates with Yvonne Holley. There were two. The first was held at the motor speedway at Charlotte in the press room. That went very well. In that debate, we focused on two things. Number one, we did not wish to appear to be bullying my opponent.

We wanted to avoid coming off as pounding this sweet older lady upside the head. We intended to highlight the difference in confidence and competence between us, and especially contrast the muddle of her various positions with the clarity of our campaign message.

Second, we wanted to communicate with the people of North Carolina, letting them know that what we offered was what they need to succeed—and that we were not about merely forking over handouts and spoils, like the Democrats. Republicans like me want you to succeed on your own because we believe in you. The audience had changed at that point from Republican to everybody, and we were aware of that. I would conclude by reminding everyone that while my opponent might appear to be a sweet, kindly grandmother, she would continue to do everything in her power to expand the welfare state, which would continue harming the very people she purported to help.

She wasn't there because she believed in you. She was there because she believed in *government*. She believed government is the solution.

We believed and still believe that *you* are the solution. We need to provide things to keep you safe and secure, but we also need to provide you the space you need to thrive and succeed on your own.

We knew we had to make this distinction, and so we hammered on it. We had to make a hard distinction between who she was and who I was. We were two people with very different philosophies that would lead to very different outcomes. We wanted people to answer these questions: Will I vote for this career politicians who wants to stay on the same old course? Or, will I vote for somebody who builds the state based on his trust in *me* and his desire for *me* to succeed?

I felt like I won that debate—and did it without attacking her.

We had another debate, but that one was done virtually. I did not like that format. In the debate, a reporter tried to attack me over some Facebook posts I'd made. It would have been different if the attack had come from my opponent. But it came from a supposedly neutral questioner.

That infuriated Conrad. He felt like it was an ambush. It did allow me to make a statement I stand by to this day: Other than my caveats about that *Black Panther* post, I don't back off anything I said on social media. I was a private citizen. I had a right to say it. You may not like it, but that's the way it works. We don't need to be talking about what I said as a private citizen on Facebook. What we need to be talking about is my opponent's record as a public servant. She has not stood up for the unborn. She has not stood up for law enforcement. The cities have been on fire. We've had riots. And now a reporter sits here and ask me about a Facebook post from years ago that maybe a hundred people saw. We're talking about the wrong things, the wrong issues.

I think that went over very well. That was a question I did not think was coming that night, but I knew it would eventually. I knew I wasn't going to back away from any of it. I got to the point where I was carrying a tissue or a handkerchief. I was ready to tell people, "If you read one of my old Facebook posts and you don't like it, then I will give you this tissue. There are four corners in this room, and you can go to one of those corners with this tissue and cry your eyes out. I don't care. The First Amendment gives me the right to say anything except fire, fire, fire, and things of that sort. You won't find me shouting fire or physically threatening anyone on my Facebook page or anywhere else. I was a private citizen delivering my political thoughts about individuals who were in office, in the limelight, and running our country, and I was either speaking about what they were doing wrong, or I was speaking through satire. Either way, if you don't like it, that's too bad."

On election night, we were at a hotel across the street from WGHP in High Point. There was a huge ballroom. Election night was very nerve-wracking. As I was looking at the returns, I was tied for most of the night. Conrad kept telling me not to worry because the red counties hadn't come in yet. I kept asking, "Have they come in, have they come in?" It wasn't going like the primary, when I was ahead all night. But they did trickle in. I can distinctly remember that I was pacing the floor, and a fellow who was working for me, Jason, a retired highway patrolman, said, "Hey, you pulled ahead."

I went to look at the screen and watched it go up. Fifty percent, then 50.5 percent, then 51. I continued to watch it. Conrad was on his computer, looking at everything, and I remember him slamming the computer closed and saying, "It's over. She does *not* have a pathway. It's over."

"Come on, are you sure?" I asked.

"She has got to call. She has got to concede. She does not have a pathway."

So I went outside with Yolanda, where I was pacing back and forth in the patio area. When the phone rang, it said "Raleigh" on it. I answered, and it was Yvonne Holley.

She conceded. We had a good conversation. She said she didn't agree with me politically, but she was glad she got to run against me and was proud of me. She said she wanted me to go out and represent the people of North Carolina well. I said, "I will." I hung up.

Yolanda looked at me and nodded. "I told you so."

We walked back inside to a little anteroom. We were all back there, family and staff. I found Conrad and told him Yvonne Holley had conceded. Everybody went nuts.

They were already out in the ballroom roaring. I walked out and gave our speech.

There were two big disappointments that night. Dan Forest didn't win at the state level. Then, of course, we know what would happen with President Trump later on at the federal level.

But we won. And though I was very disappointed that Dan Forest didn't take the governorship, it did create a clear path for what I might do next. In 2024, Democrat Roy Cooper's term will be up. People are going to be thoroughly sick of him and his failing policies. They already are.

In 2024, the Republican field in North Carolina will be open to run for governor.

21

LIEUTENANT GOVERNOR

I MET a lady in the capital the other day—a real soft-spoken lady. She walked up to me. "Are you Mark Robinson?"

I said, "Yes, ma'am."

She said, "Let me tell you. I am a Democrat, and I don't agree with a lot of the stuff that you say. But I voted for you. I voted for you because I believe in what you're saying because you believe it. I believe you'll do what's best for this state. I don't agree with you on abortion and some of these other things because I'm a liberal. But I really just have confidence in you."

I replied, "Thank you, very much."

It seemed such an odd conversation. I suppose you might call her a character voter. It is a very different way than I think about politicians. But she does have a point. Many politicians clam up when it's time for them to start talking. What matters to them are the political points they can score or the trouble they believe they are avoiding. I am not afraid to speak up when it is most crucial to speak up. Perhaps this is what stood out to the soft-spoken woman.

I think that personal opinion is not the same thing as a policy position. It's an entirely different thing. It's one thing to say, "I don't believe in gay marriage." It's another thing entirely to say that homosexual people who cohabitate together should not have the same rights that heterosexuals do. I believe wholeheartedly that if you're a homosexual couple who are legally bound, you should have those rights.

Now I'm not personally going to call it marriage because I believe that marriage is ordained between a man and a woman. I believe gay marriage is not marriage either in the eyes of God or even by definition. But that is not the same thing as going against the basic right of every individual to live their lives. If two people are a legally bound couple, then they have the right to do the same things as heterosexual people do. You can get insurance with your partner, you can leave your money to your partner (just as a heterosexual would to their spouse), and you sign over power of attorney to your partner (just as a heterosexual would to their spouse). There should not be separate legal requirements. But I don't believe you should come down to the schoolhouse, most especially the elementary schoolhouse, and teach kids about what you do in the bedroom, as if your sexual preferences and practices ought to be celebrated and given government approval and even support. That's nobody's business. It ought not to be in education, and it ought not to be in government. Those are other people's children. For your kids, you will decide what moral precepts and beliefs to teach them as a parent.

What about heterosexual sex? I don't think we ought to be teaching that in the elementary classroom either. Reading, writing, math—those belong in the classroom. Arts, music, sports? Maybe. They are adjuncts that lead to better outcomes in reading, writing, and math. Sex education does not. Kids don't have sex. They'll find out about that in the by-and-by. At that stage of their lives, they need to learn how to read at an appropriate level and to do math. There's a wall that separates children from teenagers and adults. It's built into the nature of being a kid. And to get past that wall, you either have to throw them through it or throw them over it. In either case, you risk hurting that child. The true task of a parent or teacher is to let them get old enough and tall enough to climb over that wall on their own. If you don't, you're going to do damage to them.

You have to let a child be a child. When they start moving into that adolescent realm, you can have those conversations with them, slowly. But what they are doing now is messing with those kids' minds from an early age. Telling a child, "Oh, you're gay," or dressing a kid up at the gay pride parade in a fairy costume with a pair of rainbow flags—using kids like that is demented. You shouldn't let them walk around seeing men with their butts hanging out, people dressed to show off their sexual organs, people practically naked, mimicking having sex in public. It's not good for children to be exposed to that. You wouldn't take them into a strip club or a bar full of prostitutes. They are kids. I don't understand the mentality of someone who would do that to their kids or other people's kids. "Beats everything I've seen," as Andy Griffith used to say.

* * *

Honestly, I know people in politics who are very jaded, and I now see how they became that way. I don't have sympathy for them. I don't think there's any excuse for it. But I understand.

When you are blessed to get in a position where millions of people vote for you—not thousands, not hundreds of thousands, but millions—you have an absolute obligation to do the job to the best of your ability and abide by the beliefs that got you there. Even if you're not a Christian, you still have an obligation to do some self-study in the mirror every day, to keep to your word and to remain humble. Christians have a double obligation, both to themselves and to God, to keep themselves that way by prayer, fasting, or whatever it may be. You need to do whatever it takes to keep yourself focused, to keep yourself humble. Very, very few people get the opportunity to have that kind of responsibility. And if it turns you sour, then you have not done your job.

So even though I understand, those who are jaded or even corrupt don't get a pass. If you can't handle the fame or the responsibility, you never should have taken it on. You should have stepped aside. But this is the same thing I would say about any job, for instance working in a restaurant, which I did a lot. If you're working in a restaurant and you have a bad attitude toward your customers, you need to go somewhere else and do something else. I didn't say that to anyone else first. I said that to myself first.

Are employees getting mad because a pizza phone order is hard to take, the person is hard to understand, or whatever? That's ridiculous. You're getting paid to do your job. It's human nature to get frustrated, but at some point, you have got to overcome human nature and do the right thing, take the order, and be nice about it. Or, in the case of politicians, keep doing what people voted you in to do. It's like this with everything. A man might be attracted to a good-looking woman. Human nature piques his interest. But that man also has a brain that should tell him that everything that glitters isn't gold, and a conscience that tells him about the obligations he has and about the pain he and others will face if he doesn't behave responsibly.

We are children on the floor playing. We think we're not. We think we're geniuses and grownups. Elon Musk thinks he's a genius. All the doctors studying the coronavirus think they're geniuses. And politicians think they're kings of the Earth. Business people, or football and basketball players—they all say, "We're the best! Ain't nothing ever been like us, and never will be again."

In reality, what we are is a bunch of kids at a daycare center. God is in charge of the daycare center, and he's looking at us, halfway grinning, halfway crying. If we could really see what we are compared to God, we would be stunned by our own complete misunderstanding of our position in the universe. This world we live in—that we puff ourselves up in—is not the real thing. This is all going to go away someday. This is all going to end. And we're going to go to a place afterward where the first day we wake up will be eternity. That's when things get real. While the things we do now are important down here, ultimately whatever we may think we accomplish on Earth is not really the goal. What's important is whether or not we are pleasing to God and whether the things we do are pleasing to God. And if they are not, we need to change course, no matter what we're doing, no matter how important we think it is.

That was me when I was young, wandering through life, working, goofing off, thinking I had my plan and that was it. Then God came along and said, "Nope. Put that up, boy. Time for you to do this instead." I was like a kid playing with his toy trucks and cars on the floor. And to the kid, that's his whole world. He's building a city. He's building an empire. He's driving a dangerous load across dangerous ground. He's doing surgery on his teddy bear, and it's very serious, because the teddy bear is going to die unless he can fix it.

His parents are sitting there thinking this is cute, but they know that it's a fake bear, the little boy is not really doing surgery, and when it's time to go to the store or somewhere, he will need to put the bear away and go. It's the same relationship we have with God. In the end, that's exactly what happens. No matter what you do, He's going to call you away from the toys, and you have to go along with God. Life activities are important, but only as a means to an end. We have to keep that in perspective. God and eternity are the end we're heading for. So let's focus on him. This also helps in our own lives. The more we focus on him, the less we mess up what we're doing. That's what helps us be able to do our jobs and live our lives better.

* * *

I'm still getting used to being in office, to getting a rhythm. It's been difficult because my experience as lieutenant governor has been different. None of the other people share the same story as I do. None of those folks were national figures. Trying to find a balance between staying a state figure as opposed to a national figure can be difficult. I have duties and responsibilities in North Carolina. But at the same time, one of the biggest duties of a lieutenant governor in the state is to carry the message for the party that they represent and the values they believe in. There's no better way to do that than talk about it, not just in North Carolina but on a national stage, to highlight what North Carolina is doing and what North Carolina Republicans believe and have accomplished. But it's a balancing act. I am a member of the state school board. I preside over the Senate in the North Carolina General Assembly. I chair the North Carolina Energy Policy Council. I have to take those very same values and find ways to argue for and implement them in those arenas as well. But the past few months have been a complete and total whirlwind, I have to say.

For instance, I was invited to attend the Faith and Freedom Conference in Florida this past summer, where I spoke along with Florida Governor Ron DeSantis. Some people there, such as Glenn Beck, were talking about a DeSantis/Robinson ticket in 2024. Beck said he would not be "thrilled" with the Republican Party unless he saw that. I'm very happy to fire up the base and speak my heart at such events and want to continue doing so. But I'm mostly concerned at the moment with the governance of North Carolina, which I believe needs a big change at the highest level. That's where my political energy is focused. I ran to make a difference, and I intend to do that now that the people have trusted me and believed in our message to the point of electing me.

At the moment, I'm laser focused on the executive branch of the government in North Carolina. When Richard Burr announced his retirement and that future Senate seat came up, some pressed me to declare for the position. I thought about it, but I did not. I really do feel that I am better suited to the executive branch. I want to get things done, not talk, talk, talk in Washington. I want to be able to set policy, to direct policy. That's how you really change things for the better and affect people's lives. But delivering the message and being in a bully pulpit, such as I have as lieutenant governor, is also a responsibility I take very seriously. I do think God made me the way I am with the skills that I have so I can deliver a strong message and stand up for what I believe is right. There is something to be said for inspiring others to get involved so they take a stand for what they know is true.

If some did approach me about running for a national office, it's going to sound funny or odd perhaps, but I would leave it up to God—and social media.

I would put it up on my social media and ask folks what they think I should do. That's just the way I am about this stuff. I feel comfortable on social media. Social media is where I started my political journey by making memes and posting my thoughts. When you have interesting and dedicated readers and followers, social media can provide a very good proving ground to see all sides to a decision, to work it out with logic and humor and all the other things that go on there. There are so many political implications you are asked to take into consideration; all these professional political people will come at you with these numbers and with this and that consideration. But I'd take it to my comfort zone to ruminate about it.

I would also pray about such a decision. That almost goes without saying.

I'd consider my health. I'm at the age when I need a cardiologist in the hip pocket to make sure I have somebody I can reach out to for advice on staying heart healthy. I don't have anything wrong now, but my mom had a history of heart disease. I make sure I go for periodic checkups, stay on a course of action that's heart healthy, and continue to lose weight (despite my great love for cereal!).

And, of course, I would ask Yolanda what she thought. Those would be my three factors for making a decision. It would be a very hard decision because I am quite serious about possibly running for governor of the state of North Carolina in 2024. We have had a leader who has taken us a long way in the wrong direction over the course of his two terms, and that's where I think I could be of great service to the people of this state. Somebody's got to right this ship before it sinks. While I have not declared for that race, we are making plans to make a strong run should I decide to.

22

THREE ISSUES THAT MATTER
MOST TO THE NATION

THE SUMMER OF 2020 was a crazy time to campaign, with COVID-19 and BLM riots. But these things bolstered my campaign. As time went on and things got worse, as protests turned to riots and became extremely violent, my message got even bolder. The things I'd been talking about came alive. It was like the destructive memes popped right out of Facebook, with people like BLM and antifa running around. And that year, New York state came out with partial birth abortion legislation that legalized abortion up to the point of birth, or even *after*. It was unbelievable, positively demonic. People were cheering in the New York legislature when this passed—cheering the killing of babies. That bolstered my message even more. We have to stop this craziness, this evil behavior. These people are not sane. They're not talking about aborting a child after a rape or anything like that. They're talking about *infanticide*. It's the same people who are pushing Planned Parenthood. They are not reasonable at all.

As far as BLM goes, there's no better argument for supporting law enforcement. BLM made the case. There's no better reason for supporting the police than an angry BLM activist trying to bang down *your* door and burn down *your* place of business because of what some bad-apple cop did in Minnesota. You haven't done a thing in the world, and they're at your door threatening you and your family. There's also no better argument for the Second Amendment and the lawful possession of firearms. What's more, this activity strikes at the heart of the Constitution itself when you have reporters going on television— reporters who are college educated—and saying things like, "Where does the law say, the Constitution say, that protest has to be peaceful?"

Protest is by definition the exercise of the right found in First Amendment, freedom of speech. Violence—hurting other people and burning down places—is not an exercise of free speech. That is the opposite. It's preventing others from exercising their right to expression, depriving them of a forum, of a livelihood—and sometimes, as we saw in Portland and other places, of life itself. Murder—that's not protest—that's rioting and mayhem. You're trying to force people to do what you want, not reason with them or convince them. Those journalists excusing such behavior are idiots.

Look at what they are doing to the military: CRT, transgender surgery paid for by the American taxpayer, and dismantling our American military based on this stupid "woke-ism." I have nothing but contempt for it.

These are national issues. People have similar concerns, similar longings for freedom. Abortion is an issue nationwide. It's the same issue everywhere because there's a clear divide on either side of it. Talking about abortion in North Carolina is the same as talking about it in Florida or California. It's about right and wrong, good and bad. Those categories apply everywhere. If I'm in New York City, I'm going to tell people the exact same thing I feel about abortion and what we ought to do to stop this killing of children. They *are* unborn children. I believe abortion is a sin. I believe it is not right. It needs to be ended, certainly not permitted and encouraged by law. I'll never back away from that.

Even if we were somehow able to end abortion, making it illegal tomorrow, it's still going to be part of the national conversation. The

Second Amendment and the Constitutional process is in the same position. Look at how the 2021 Democratic-sponsored bill HR 1 sought to subvert the Constitution by taking away the rights of states to have their own laws concerning their elections. It strikes right at the heart of the Constitution. The federal government is so out of control because politicians fail to realize that the Constitution is not in place to limit the powers of the people but to limit the power of the federal government.

When it comes to education and the federal government, my message is this: the federal government needs to get the hell out of education. This is the bottom line: show me in the Constitution where it says the federal government should have its nose in the way states administer education and that it should be browbeating them with federal dollars to carry out whatever it wants them to do. The Constitution does not say that. It's not the federal government's business. That's not what it's supposed to do.

It's not any different for the people of North Carolina than Virginia or Florida. We still live under the same Constitution. We still live under the same ideas that are the foundation of the Constitution. But there were times when we had to speak to specific groups to find out what their issues were. If you go out east, they have different issues than people in the mountains. And both of those areas have different issues than a lot of folks in Charlotte or Winston-Salem, and other places. It's more a matter of listening to others in those situations and finding out their concerns.

Here are what I believe are the defining issues facing our country. If I were ever to seek national office, these are the issues you would hear me talking about.

THE RIGHT TO LIFE AND OPPOSING ABORTION

I wasn't always 100 percent pro-life. I wrestled with that. I used to think of an unborn child as a "pre-baby." But as I began to grow spiritually, I came to understand that my words were just that—mere words. A pre-baby is a *baby*. And a baby is a human being.

Abortion is now one of the things that I just cannot tolerate. I find it morally wrong, and those who advocate for it are morally reprehensible. Abortion might have been legal my entire life, but I will always believe it is immoral.

For those who think abortion is morally justified, for those who like to "shout their abortion," I have this to say: when you talk to me about abortion, you'd best not bring up rape and incest. These are side issues. Even the notoriously pro-abortion Guttmacher Institute's research has claims that one percent of abortions are obtained in cases of rape—a percentage that holds steady across decades of data.[1] The percentages of abortions for these reasons are tiny in comparison to the total number of abortions. The vast, vast majority of abortions have nothing to do with rape or incest. What we're talking about is Planned Parenthood telling young women and young men that if they decided they wanted to "do their thing, with their thing," and now are pregnant and are not "ready" to have a baby, then it's okay for them to kill that child.

No, it's not. That's murder. People who do that are murdering a human being because that human being is inconveniencing them, whether it be going to college, traveling to Europe, being a vagabond, or whatever it is. They're murdering a person because the person is standing in their way and keeping them from doing something they want to do. It's no different than, for instance, me killing my neighbor because he's standing in the way of me having a job that I want.

"That guy's got a job I want, so I'm going to kill him and get that job. I'm due that job."

To me, spiritually, abortion is no different.

They are killing an innocent human being who did nothing wrong, did nothing to put them in situation they don't like. That unborn human being is not guilty of anything. They're killing that baby because it is unwanted and inconvenient. Legally, there might be a difference.

---

1   Ryan T. Anderson and Alexandra DeSanctis, *Tearing Us Apart: How Abortion Harms Everything and Solves Nothing*, Regnery Publishing, June 2022.

Even if abortion were made illegal, a lawyer might be able to argue for calling it manslaughter. But in God's eyes, murder is the intentional killing of a human being, and murder is murder.

In this country we have accepted the fact that if people don't want their baby, they can kill the baby. That's how we got to New York, to that cheering on the legislative floor over the ability to kill infants. It's a slippery slope from saying "You don't want your baby, that's okay. Get rid of your baby. We'll dispose of it, don't worry. In fact, we'll tear it into pieces, and we'll sell the parts and make a lot of money," to standing up and hollering in approval at a law that sanctions partial birth abortion. It's no wonder. That's what happens if people set the standard saying that it is okay.

They are not only harming the baby—killing it—but they are harming themselves. Many people who have had abortions deeply regret having them. Then there's the spiritual aspect. We devalue life so much by killing the truly innocent that we are raising a generation that doesn't respect life at all. We see people get shot over video games or over some minor drug deal. Kids are going to school and shooting their classmates because they got picked on. Why do these kids disrespect human life so much? We're living in a society now where the most innocent lives are not respected and where taking those lives is not only allowed but celebrated in some places, such as the New York legislature. Abortion is a root cause of many of our society's problems.

You can be hard pressed to make that connection with people. Many are just unwilling to believe this is the case. But when people don't respect life at its beginning, at its most vulnerable, how can you expect to have a generation of children who will respect life at all? Many don't—because we're *telling* them not to.

The world is full of people walking around with bad mouths and bad breath, offending us, saying things we don't like, maybe even taunting us and making us mad. If someone doesn't respect an innocent baby, why should they respect another person's life? Just because they are human beings, God's creation? If we can't respect the life of a baby, we're not going to respect some offensive guy's life. But if people do respect life, human life in the womb, then someone may think twice before resorting to violence. This jackass is somebody's child, someone's brother or sister, or maybe someone's father or mother. Who are we to take their life? People should respect that life, even if they don't respect that person. It all begins by respecting the innocent. We've got to get back to that as a society. The more vicious forms we allow this disrespect of life to take, the more we will see degenerate, horrible behavior.

This is why I am so strongly pro-life and opposed to abortion. It's why I talk about it in almost every speech I give, even when some people would rather I drop it, let it be, and talk about other issues. I'm hard pressed to get people to agree that legalized abortion has these terrible effects on society that I see so clearly, but I'm not going to give up bringing it up and calling it out.

EDUCATION

I absolutely hate the attempt to racialize history and education with the so-called 1619 Project and critical race theory. For all conservatives—Rush Limbaugh, me, Larry Elder, Candace Owens—this is the embodiment of things we've been warning about, screaming from the rafters about, for years. We said it was coming down the pike, and here it is.

But the biggest problem with public education in America right now is the sheer ineptitude and incomprehensibility embodied in our pedagogical philosophy.

I sit in North Carolina State Education Board meetings, listen to them yammer, yammer, yammer, and think every time, "What the hell does any of this mean?"

When I complain they'll say something that implies that I don't understand the nuances of educating children, so my opinion doesn't matter.

Let me tell you something: education is a simple proposition. We didn't have one kid in our daycare center who needed something *different* from the tried and true to learn the ABCs. There wasn't one kid that I had to take aside and say "Well, I need to figure out how to teach you the ABCs in some way different from the tried-and-true practice of drawing them, writing them, and saying them."

The educrats want to make it a complicated bureaucracy so that ordinary people are repulsed and don't get involved.

Dr. Terry Stoops said it the best: "Education standards should be written so they can be handed to the average layperson and such a person can read and understand them."

When ordinary people finish reading a standard, they should not be thinking, "What the heck did that just say? What is all this?"

My belief is this: If you're such a high falutin' egghead genius, if you're the smartest man in the room, why can't you communicate with the person you think is the dumbest person in the room? That should be easy for you. If you can't communicate with the dumbest person in the room, you are not the smartest person in the room. In fact, you might be the dumbest person in the room. If you can't connect with somebody who only has a seventh-grade education and if you can't help them—don't tell me you're smart. The smartest guy in the room can talk to everybody and wants to learn from others to get even smarter.

A lot of times in those state school board meetings, I just want to raise my hand and say, "Why don't y'all speak English instead of 'edu-ese'?"

Parents are utterly fed up. That's why so many charter schools and private schools are opening up. People are sick of wasting money. More than forty percent of the state budget is spent on education.

And the Democrats and their bureaucrats are always complaining, "We need more money, more money."

You need to call a lean manufacturing person into the boards.

Divide up the room into two groups and tell one group they can go home. We don't know what you're going to do, but you don't work for us anymore. You're released from your duties. You're the smartest people around. I'm sure you'll figure something out, just like Wile E. Coyote. Buy yourself some rocket skates. Go chase a roadrunner."

Education isn't about whitewashing history. It's not possible to teach history without talking about the bad things that happened. We must look at the impact that slavery had on our economy, social structure, our government, and the dreadful effects that it had on the people themselves. We have to look at how odd it was that a nation built on freedom had slaves.

We need to stop demonizing people based on their color, and we need to stop telling people that they are victims based on the color of their skin. We need to start telling them that they are Americans, and the way we as Americans overcame these injustices was by using our unique system of government. That's what conservatives are trying to get taught. We aren't trying to hide anything. We don't want to whitewash anything. We want to teach the real story, and the real story is this—yes, we had injustices, but we overcame those things together. We can still do that.

Teachers can get to the great issues of our time and philosophy of life later. If they teach kids how to read, they teach kids how understand information and how to consider concepts. If they teach kids how to write, they teach kids how to communicate. If they teach kids math, they teach kids to think logically and scientifically. This is what elementary kids want and need, and it is *all* that they truly need. Every activity in school, including art, music, and other activities, should be directed toward that goal.

Of course, children will succeed at different levels, but the expectation and concentration should be to allow children to ascend to the highest level that they are capable of. We don't need to dumb things down; we need to smarten them up. The way to do this is to demand proficiency in reading, writing, and math in grades one through five. In those grades, we don't need to be teaching social studies. We don't need to be teaching science. We surely don't need to be talking about equity and social justice. I'll say it again: we need to be teaching kids how to read, how to write, and how to do mathematics.

If I were totally in charge of education, that's the course I would set.

it in North Carolina. Even though I sit on the state school board now, I would get rid of it. We need to have one entity, one person, where the buck stops. Right now we have at least three: the school boards, the state superintendent of education, and the local school systems—and none are truly answerable to the others. We need for one entity to be in charge of education in the state so that when the legislature has questions and concerns, they can go to that single institution and expect to influence the way education is done. They could ask one person, "What in the world is going on? Why and how is this happening? How are you going to fix it?" Right now in North Carolina—it's a mess. The buck needs to stop with somebody.

Of course, the basic policies of education should be determined by local school boards. We're working on getting good people in those positions. That's as important as rationalizing the state oversight.

The kids that come out the best are not the ones who merely obtain proficiency. We need to expect more. The kids who do the best? They can read some Greek and Latin. They can understand Shakespeare.

Let's face it, this is roleplay, fantasyland. In reality, we will have to prioritize. We will have to look at the most pressing issues. What might they be? They include misplaced federal involvement in local education, the mishmash of appointees and hired people who set state policy, and the intransigence and blackmail of the teachers' union. We must decide which is the most pressing, given the present circumstances, and start working on changing that one thing. I've said this often: it's not going to be an overnight fix, and I can't fix it by myself in North Carolina. It will take a concentrated effort over a number of years. It's going to take likeminded people who are bound and determined to see our education system get back to where it was—because we have fallen far—and then to where it needs to be.

The problems in our system didn't happen overnight and won't be repaired overnight. It's just like my being over three hundred pounds. I didn't get this way overnight, and I can't take a pill and be a hundred and eighty-six pounds overnight. But the way to change things is to identify the biggest obstacle, and take that down first, taking it step by step, being determined and not backing off, because there are powerful institutional forces set against us, frozen in place and determined never to budge. It's not going to be easy. We also need to capitalize on success when we achieve it. We need voucher programs to get students into the best schools possible. We need more charter schools replicating the one that people are lined up to get into. We need to build more, not limit them.

And if we find success along the way, we should bring it into the system. We might adopt charter school methods throughout the system. We might see a mass exodus from the public schools entirely, and before you know it, traditional public schools might be a thing of the past. We should go with what works and what produces the base: those good citizens and students prepared for the working life of an American when they graduate.

Higher education also must change. We give out so much money in student aid and subsidized loans, but the one thing we don't ask is if the students have a plan concerning what they will do when they graduate and how they are going to pay that loan money back. This is not to say they must decide on a career for all time. But they must be serious about repaying the money they borrow for their education and have an idea of how they are going to do so. If I go to a bank and ask for a million dollar loan to start a business, the first thing they'll want to see is my plan. How will I make this business a success? We ought to do the same thing with federal money given to students. How will the student get through school? What goals are they going to set to get to where they want to be on the other side? How are they going to pay the loan back? Can't show any of this? They don't get the money. A little responsibility like this would go a long way to making students much more serious about their education.

23

THREE MORE ISSUES THAT

MATTER MOST TO THE NATION

VETERANS AND THE MILITARY

It's an issue of what's right. Think about veterans who have served twenty years and have served in combat. When they come home and the government is talking about giving out any entitlements, their names need to be on top of the list. Give them what they've earned. Give them the respect they've earned. What incentive does a young man or young woman have to join the military when they watch veterans come home and be mistreated? They may have been grievously wounded and can't even get the care that they deserve and have earned. What do young people learn when they see veterans mistreated by the very government that sent them over to fight for and defend us? It's not right, and it's a terrible message. It's also a matter of who we respect in this nation. When Michael Jordan walks into the room, everybody goes crazy. Larry, your neighbor, shuffles into the room with that cap that says Vietnam Veteran, a man who perhaps fought at Khe Sanh, and nobody notices. People know he fought, but most don't even know what happened. "Oh, that's just old Larry." It's a matter of who we have respect for in this nation.

People walk among us who have done things no player in the NBA, no Hollywood actor, would ever even consider doing. They did those things not to become enriched, but for honor. If we don't have any veterans, we aren't going to have a nation. If the government has money for recruiting, training, and equipment, it must have money for taking care of veterans. They are just as essential, maybe more so, because they bring the defense of the nation back to society. The bean counters should worry about other things instead of limiting veterans' benefits. If the government is a little short, the last thing to be sacrificed should be our veterans' needs. "Can't get you those artificial leg gaskets, can't get you that treatment. Maybe next month. Here's some red tape to cut through while you're waiting." This should never happen. Veterans are our connection to the military that ensures the survival of this country. They are inspirational just by existing.

Gender reassignment surgery—I can't believe we are discussing having the military, and taxpayers, pay for this.

Should the VA pay for this? No. I'll be honest with you. People who are transgender should not be in the military. I don't believe they are mentally stable. If people don't know if they are a man or a woman—if they want to do that, that's their right. But do that somewhere else. They can find out who they are somewhere else. It's like saying, "Today I want to chop off my left foot. My left foot's gotta go. But I also want to stay in the Army." No. If people want to chop off their foot, well, they do have a right to mutilate themselves. I would suggest that they should not do that. But they can go ahead if they insist. It's their right, as surely as it is their body. But being in the military takes a special person, someone more concerned with others than self. People aren't going to chop their feet off in the US Marine Corp. Not in the Army, Navy, Coast Guard, or Space Force. Not even in the Air Force. And we must not encourage and pay for gender reassignment surgery with taxpayer money. It is detrimental to the mission. If people insist on going down this route, they need to get out of the military as soon as they can and pay for it themselves.

I am appalled by the wrongheadedness of the leaders in charge of national defense, who have so lost their way as to want to pay for something like gender reassignment surgery. What are they doing? Do they not understand how important what they do, what they are charged with the care of, is to the rest of us? People get mad at my position and say: "You're a bigot. You're a homophobe. You don't understand."

I do understand. I'm saying that someone who is troubled in this way has something wrong with their brain. I'm not saying they don't have a right to be part of society. I'm not saying they can't express themselves the way they want to express themselves. I'm not saying we should hunt them down and beat them with sticks or purge them from our neighborhoods. I'm only saying that this condition disqualifies them from the United States military. We do not need people with those types of issues serving.

People need to be at 100 percent capacity to serve in what is the most vital role of the US government. We have lowered our standards. We are in a dangerous place.

The military is unlike anything else. It must have very high standards. There are plenty of changes that can be made for the good that will bring the standards up. This is why Executive Order 9981 issued in 1948 was so important. This order integrated the US military. Integration of the military *raised* the military's standards. Justice or societal change was secondary, of little importance in comparison. I can also remember, years ago, when there was the argument over whether gay people should be in the military. I remember thinking to myself, "You guys are a little late. They're already here—and have been the whole time."

I don't care what the organization is, there are gay people in it. People should best believe it, whether it's the church or the military. Should gay people be there? Perhaps that's a conversation to be had. But whenever that conversation happens, we often encounter the one person who wants to bring in the transgender issue. "What about a man who wants to be a woman, or vice versa?" He might want to be a refrigerator. It's not going to happen. This is a mental problem, not a fact of life, and certainly not something the military should be concerned with. Gay people in the military are a whole different ball of wax. They are not confused about whether they are a man or woman. They just do something different in the bedroom, and it's nobody's business what anyone does in the bedroom. Being gay does not interfere with the mission.

Furthermore, if I am getting on a plane to go somewhere and the pilot is obviously transgender—well, I'm getting off. If someone is confused about the basics of their humanity, they probably shouldn't be flying an airplane. Call me a bigot, or call me judgmental. Judgment is how we make it through life. Judgment is about treating natural differences fairly and not ignoring mental problems people have, especially if their problems could result in harm to others. Again, people can cut off their hands if they want to. If they insist, I may help them to make it less dangerous. Tie it off, coat the spot with betadine, and put the saw blade in boiling water. But if someone cuts off their hand and come to me looking for work as a carpenter? No. I'm not going to hire that person, and I shouldn't.

We're going to get our military back in shape. We have to. Our lives depend on it.

Now you may think what follows is silly or trivial, but I assure you I am serious. Speaking as a young man who was attracted to the military, who couldn't wait to join, I will explain how you get the best of the best in our armed forces.

It comes down to pride. It comes down to people taking pleasure in being the best at something or striving until they are. It comes down to respect for the uniform—literal respect.

We need to stop letting these men and women walk around in Battle Dress Uniforms (BDUs) and unshined shoes. We need to get them back into uniforms they can be proud of. We need to get our training standards up so we can be world class. I'm sorry, but we won't be cutting anybody any slack just so they can be part of the military. The military is going to be made up of world-class individuals, and if someone is not world class, they can go somewhere else. If people can't pass the physical tests, if they can't pass the mental tests, they can't join. People can't be part of the infantry if they can't shoot, jump, and run. Someone can't be a Ranger just because they want to be. This is not a social justice outfit.

The military was integrated long ago because integration strengthened the military and hence strengthened the country. Anybody who is going to be fighting for the freedom of this country needs to be world class and meet the highest standards. I'm extremely passionate about this. Somebody needs to step up and get our military back to where it was, not just in equipment, but in morale and competence. I get distressed every time I see soldiers walking through the airport wearing BDUs. If I had walked through an airport in BDUs when I was in the military, I'd have gotten my ass kicked by my superiors. We didn't do that.

When you went to the airport, you had on Class As or Class Bs. You had those shoes shined and those pants pressed. You were representing the United States of America and something greater than yourself, the idea of this nation. That's not so anymore, at least by appearances. The standards have gone way down. It's a shame. And today we see this wave of woke-ism slipping into the military. Commanding officers claim that the biggest threat to our country is—climate change? The most populous country in the world, China is waiting to come over here and take everything we've got, but commanding officers tell me that climate change is the biggest threat? That focus should definitely shift.

And people talk about veterans. Of course we talk about veterans' care and doing right by our soldiers and veterans. But we also need to bring the US military back to a place where it is the premiere military in the world.

When people see a soldier, they should say, "Wow, *that's* a United States Army soldier." "Wow, *that's* a United States Marine," "Wow, *that's* an airman," or "Wow, *that's* a sailor."

Standards need to be the absolute highest. It's a shame when basketball and football teams have higher physical standards than the military has for the men and women who protect our nation in the US armed forces.

I'm not saying that everybody in the armed forces needs to be a super-soldier, but certainly those who serve need to meet standards that will set them apart. It should not just be lip service, but something one must work for. And I believe if we do that, we'll make people proud to be part of the organization and always get the best of the best. We won't struggle to get people to join the military. People won't look at the military as "less than." People will say, "Hey, I want to be a part of that. And I'm going to work hard to be part of it," just like they might say they would work hard to become a part of the NBA or NFL.

I see these videos that show guys returning from deployment, and they go to the school or church or wherever and come out of a giant box or birthday cake or whatever in those BDUs. Other than the son or daughter, who will be very happy because their daddy is home, what other kid is going to look at that guy popping out and say "Wow"? He's just some guy in a wrinkled set of dungarees and a pair of old dusty boots. They haven't been shined because they can't be shined. No one would look at that and say, "Well, gee, I want to be him. I want to wear that prison garb he's got on." It's distressing. Here's one of the secrets to make people want to join the military: shiny brass buttons, pressed uniforms, a sense of pride in this appearance, and the esprit de corps that was always part of the military. I feel this has now been lost, dissipated.

What does this do to make better soldiers? When I was in JROTC, one thing I wanted more than anything was to get berets for the drill team and color guard. Our sergeant major was dead set against it. He did not want to do it. I believe he was thinking that I wanted something like what AYD dance teams wore, headdresses haphazardly canted on their noggins.

That's not what I wanted. I had seen guys in the special forces wearing berets. They had the lining torn out and pressed flat against the side of the head, with the flash pulled forward. That's just so sharp. And it represented their excellence, their accomplishments, their sense of belonging to an elite organization. I told the sergeant major, "If we get those berets and we wear them right, we will really set ourselves apart.

You'll see our drill team explode. We're going to be able to pick and choose who joins the drill team, who joins the color guard. We're not going to have to beg people to join. People are going to flock toward us and want to be part of us."

And doggone if it wasn't true. We got those berets and cut the linings out of them. We would meet after school, stand at the mirror, and get them the way we wanted them, then we would iron them and press them, and position our flash on them just right. I can still remember the first time we wore them. We wore maroon berets and walked through school. Of course, there were some naysayers, some goofy idiots joshing us about it. But they were joshing because they were envious and jealous. Before long, people were coming to us because we were set apart, elite, sharp. Look at that beret; that says it all! Not only that, more people started joining ROTC. Shiny brass, cords on our arms, pressed uniforms—people would look at those things and say, "I want to be part of that. I want to look like that. I want to walk down the hall and have people look at me that way."

Consider the Marines. There is no place you can go in the world where people don't recognize a US Marine. It's the sharpest uniform on the planet. You're not going to find any military uniform anywhere that can hold a candle to Marine Corp dress blues.

That uniform is known all around the world because of the excellence it represents. It looks heroic. It causes the wearer to want to live up to that standard, too.

I think that in large measure our military is starting to lose this. The Marines are not losing it as much, but the Army definitely is. I really think we need to get it back.

FOREIGN POLICY

Even though I am only the lieutenant governor of North Carolina, believe it or not, I do have a foreign policy prescription for those entrusted with the safety of these United States in the world.

Read history.

The way to react to foreign events, to plan and be proactive for what is to come, or to face those threats and opportunities our country might experience, is to go back and look through history and take lessons from it.

When I was in the Army, what did we hear about? One word: Russia! Russia, Russia, Russia. Russia was the enemy. We learned about Russian weapons. We learned how to identify Russian tanks. Now were we in a state of war with the Russians? No. But we were preparing ourselves for a state of war so we could avoid one. We were training, making sure that we were ready in case of war with Russia.

Russia is still a problem, no doubt. Russia is in economic decline and the encroachment of neighbors who side with Western countries has caused them lash out in brutal fashion. But China is a new global near-peer competitor to our country and, ultimately, more worrisome. We should sit down and tell the Chinese that we want peace and that we'll do whatever we can to maintain peace. But make no mistake: the Chinese should know if they do something to threaten our vital interests or the vital interest of our allies or if they attack us militarily, they might as well stack up their body bags. We're not going to hold back a bit. We're going to be ready.

So we need to prepare for war with China not because we seek war—far from it—but because the Chinese Communist Party has made itself, practically *declared* itself, our enemy. Some might say, "Well, this will just provoke them into war."

It doesn't work like that. Have people not been paying attention to what communists do? We saw it in Korea. We saw it in Vietnam. We see it in places in Latin America. Communists like to invade people's countries. Then after they invade the country, they like to kill the people. They don't view people as important, only their precious state. We can't let that happen. Why are we not doing everything we can to defend ourselves from China? Why is the military worried about woke-ism, instead of China?

Our country needs to wake up on national defense. We are not taking it seriously enough in our minds or our hearts. We have to show foresight and courage. We are not taking the threat from China earnestly enough. Look at the rapidly development of Chinese weapons. Does their array of weapons seem familiar? Many of them are direct copies of American weapons made with stolen plans and blueprints—or worse, with technology we willingly transferred.

Then look at history. Look at Japan. Why did they become what they became during World War II?

Because they were trying to emulate the West, the United States in particular. They didn't get it right, not for a while. But they eventually did.

When Japan was a closed society that wouldn't let anyone in, the US sent emissaries there trying to make contact and establish trade. No dice. The US finally pushed them to open up by sending a military armada of ships to Tokyo Bay. On July 8, 1853, American Commodore Matthew Perry took four ships into the bay.

Perry didn't attack. That was not the point. He showed them ships that were far more advanced than anything the Japanese had. Then he came back the next spring with even more.

The Japanese rulers saw this and were intimidated. They lost face. Japanese technology seemed primitive in comparison to Perry's ships. The leadership realized they had to adapt. They didn't get the right idea at first. "Maybe we need to do what the Europeans do and build an empire, and that will lead to greatness." What they didn't get right at the time was democracy. For a while, the Japanese plan worked. They started on a course of modernizing, creating a mechanized military. They had a chance to try out their military against the Russians in the Russo-Japanese war. And they had a stunning victory against the Russians at Port Arthur. It was a proto–Pearl Harbor style of attack. They surprised the Russians and forced them to capitulate.

This bolstered their confidence even more, and they began to expand their empire, to keep expanding. And in that expansion, one of the things they did was to send people to the United States to study.

In the years before World War II, many Japanese military commanders came to the US, hobnobbed with American military commanders, and talked to them about tactics and strategy. Meanwhile, they were studying the population, determining weak points, and understanding our psychology—or so they thought. In the 1920s and 1930s, there was an explosion of Japanese culture in America, and vice versa in Japan. There was a quasi-bonding. But it was an uneasy relationship.

Japan was not a democracy. It was hell-bent on building an empire and taking over other countries and other places. They believed that government, the emperor's chosen, could decide what should be done. And as Japan continued her quest to expand, what happened?

Their desire to expand ran into US interests in the Far East. Once those two countries collided, it was almost inevitable that their relationships would get contentious and things would come to a head, and they did in World War II.

When I was young, I didn't understand why World War II veterans were so antagonistic toward Japan. They couldn't stand seeing a Toyota on the road. They couldn't abide a Japanese steakhouse opening up. One man I went to church with, Eddy McClaine, put his son out of the house when he bought a Toyota.

WWII in the Pacific was a vicious war. It took many years for those men to get over that, and some never did. With events such as the Bataan Death March in their memory, how could anyone blame them?

Later, after World War II, the Japanese did grasp democracy and became very good at it. It was the one piece of the puzzle they had lacked. Now they are a modern democratic nation and our ally.

This is a problem with the Far East, particularly China. They don't realize that what they see in America is not part of some gigantic state plan. Our economic strength, our cultural dominance, is not some sinister ruse. Nobody strategizes and enacts it. Or, rather, everybody does all at once. It just happens because of democracy and the free market. That's also the reason China can't replicate it but has to try to steal it. But this reaction still makes China dangerous. Weapons have changed. A future war could be much worse than Pearl Harbor and the war in the Pacific.

LAW ENFORCEMENT

We warned that if the left keeps demonizing law enforcement, we would have cops quitting left and right, and crime would go through the roof. And what's happened? Cops are resigning. Defund the police? The crime rate is exploding. Now Democrats and left-wing ideologues act as if they can't figure out why. They have listened to me and to Rush Limbaugh. Or to their own common sense. It's got to be in there somewhere.

Police officers are the absolute backbone of civilized society. The same people who tell me they don't like cops are often the ones who have had an encounter that didn't go the way they wanted. "The cop pulled me over and was rude to me, and it felt threatening." I ask, "Well, what did you do?" The person replies, "I was speeding. Yeah, I was speeding, but he didn't have to talk to me like I'd done something wrong. That's not such a bad crime." That person *did* do something wrong. They're like a little kid. I know what the speed limit is, and that person knows what the speed limit is. The engineers who built the road took a look around and saw there were houses, families, and business nearby. The engineers understood that thirty-five miles an hour was a safe speed to drive that would protect other people from cars. That person wanted to speed because, well, because they *wanted* to. And if they get stopped by the police, it's their fault? Not in their minds.

Defund the police! Disrespect law enforcement and call them all racists! Nonsense. If we don't have police officers, we won't have a civilized society. We'll be back to the days of the Old West where in order to protect themselves, people had to tote around a gun and be prepared to use it at any time. Criminals take full advantage when they see cops held back and kept from being able to do anything. We have this happening today. We have entire areas where crime's been allowed to run rampant.

We've seen rioters walking around New York and throwing water

WE ARE THE MAJORITY!

on policemen, knowing the cops won't do anything and can't respond. People are throwing water on people who are armed and sworn, and *do* have the right to kill in certain circumstances. If those people are throwing water on and being disrespectful to policemen, what in the world do you think they would be willing to do to *you*? To an unarmed, frail grandpa? Or a grandma walking down the street who has a few dollars in her pocket that they want? Some people who normally wouldn't commit crimes see such things happen with no consequences, and they think, "Well, I'll do the same thing." Packs of kids are going in the stores of California, just taking whatever they want to take. They know the cops won't show up or won't do anything. They aren't allowed to. Those events in California are perfect laboratory experiments, perfect examples of civilization crumbling.

I say, "You ain't got no police, you're going to be messed up." Crime, crime, crime will follow as the night follows the day. Politicians need to stand behind law enforcement. Law enforcement is the first line of defense on the street. The first line of defense for police are elected officials. If they don't defend the people who give us law and order, it's like stabbing policemen in the back.

Now imagine you are the black mayor of a big city when some George Floyd–type thing happens there. Imagine that an average black politician comes out and says, "Hold on here. I know one police officer may have done this. But y'all can go on and cancel that noise about how you're against all these other police officers. My police officers do a great job. This one bad one? We're going to make sure we take care of him and put him away for a very long time. But we can't have all this anti-police stuff. It's bad for the community. It's bad for us, not for them. We are the ones who suffer when law enforcement is run down."

That would go a long way to achieving real justice. But by and large, that's not what you have in the cities. You have politicians who do the opposite. It's not politically expedient.

Well, I won't put up with it. And neither will most people. If anyone shows up on my doorstep trying to hurt me or my family, I'm going to kill them if necessary. Here's a secret: the police are protecting the criminals from *us*. We will defend ourselves. It's only because the police are there that we don't have to do it for ourselves and take the law into our own hands. That's how I was raised. I was raised not to bother anybody, not to lay my hands on anybody, but to defend myself if somebody tried to hurt me.

Criminals should appreciate the police. With the police, criminals get a warning. They get handcuffs. They get a magistrate, a court date, a trial, and appeals. With me or another invaded homeowner, what do they get? An AR-15 and a bullet. Or even better, a shotgun and a shotgun blast.

Defund the police? That's madness! We will see a lot of people start to shoot back and fight back. We will see businesses close. We don't need that. We don't need society to fall apart and civilization to crumble. So much of that can be solved simply by backing law enforcement and helping law enforcement to continue to improve themselves and their communities.

Whenever people see things like what happened with George Floyd, they should not see it as a call to demonize the police, but as a call to get into the police force and say, "What do you need to make sure we don't get this again? What hat do you need to make sure we don't have another ass-hat like this get through?" The elected officials should support the police, work with them to get better, and always to have their backs. We understand that there was a bad apple, and we must do everything we can to find the bad apples and make sure that doesn't happen again. But the profession is too important to be done away with because of a case like this. We need more and better policing, not less. If a hospital has one doctor who is terrible, who is incompetent, they have to deal with that doctor. They have to get rid of one bad doctor. People don't defund the entire medical profession because of the egregious acts of one doctor! We should not do this with law enforcement either. If we do, we're headed for chaos.

When someone says things like this, the antifa nutcases will call them names. And if they are black, these will be specific names.

I like it when people call me Uncle Tom. Sometimes I get called Uncle Tom and Uncle Ruckus, the guy from the *Boondocks* cartoon.

I remember one guy saying, "You're either Uncle Tom or Uncle Ruckus. Which one are you?" I replied, "I don't know. Take your pick, what do you think I am?" "Well, I think you're both of them." The people he was with laughed at this.

I looked at him and said, "The fact you called me those names proves to me you don't read classic novels but just watch cartoons. Do you even know who Uncle Tom is?"

Of course, he didn't know. When people call you that, it proves their ignorance. If those people knew the character of Uncle Tom in *Uncle Tom's Cabin*, they'd know that calling me Uncle Tom was akin to calling me Jesus Christ. In later stage productions, the character was sometimes twisted into a stereotype that Harriet Beecher Stowe wouldn't have recognized or supported. In the novel, he's a good man. I'm striving to be someone who stands up as an example to the people around him. That's what Uncle Tom did in that novel.

But the way I really answer the question is this: Who do you consider the bad person? Is it the person looking at the few instances of police brutality? Or the person looking at the massive amounts of gang violence, the massive amount of senseless killing going on in black neighborhoods? If anyone gets those statistics and lines them up beside each other, they're not even comparable.

When people talk about Breonna Taylor and George Floyd, I like to ask them, "Give me the name of one Negro killed in your community by another Negro. Give me one name."

Nine times out of ten they can't do it. But people are getting killed all around them in their neighborhood and are being murdered all around over senselessness. People are getting killed because they're on the wrong block or over some dope. These are idiotic reasons for ending lives.

They won't be able to name any of those people. They know George Floyd's name. They know Breonna Taylor's name. But they can't tell me the name of the guy who lives down the street from them and was shot last night by the gang. They can't tell me the name of the nine-year-old who got killed over at the McDonald's.

Police brutality is like a headache. This is what I mean: If you have a headache, what's going on? You don't know because it could be several things, like tension. Someone might have had a stressful day because they've been talking to liberals all day. A headache might be a migraine that could become much more severe, almost blinding, something a person needs a prescription for. Or a headache could be a brain tumor.

Brutality could just be one police officer who's a bad apple. It could be caused by a number of police officers who have banded together for bad purposes, and we need to root them out as a group. It could be a situation where the chief is bad. We need to get rid of him. Or there could be a system-wide problem that's destroying the unit. No matter which one it is, no matter what kind of headache someone might have, we can't ignore it. It must be dealt with. But it is only a symptom.

But here's the cancer, and we know it's a cancer: the genocidal rate at which black people are killing their neighbors. Why is nobody on the national stage talking about that? Why is it that every time I bring it up, or Candace Owen brings it up, or Larry Elder brings it up, the first thing out of some people's mouth is "Shut up, Uncle Tom." Could it be that the people calling us names have a vested interest in a continuing epidemic of black people killing each other? They must. It is the only conclusion one can draw.

No activist organization can ever take the place of the family. This is just as true among black folks as with any other group. The key to reforming our system of justice is to support families. That's the only cure for the genocidal cancer afflicting us. A child is better off with a mother and a father in the house, in a neighborhood where crime, great or small, is not ignored but dealt with swiftly. We are better off when the unborn and most vulnerable are protected, and when the sacrifices of our protectors are respected and celebrated. We need to stop those with a vested interest in our failure from burning down our neighborhoods or destroying them in more insidious ways. Most of all, we must shore up, rebuild when necessary, and maintain the American family. That is the bedrock upon which everything else stands.

24

THE FUTURE

THERE ARE A LOT of people out there who are fertile ground for protecting and carrying on our great republic. These ideas are like seeds. What they can become, what they can grow into, I can't say. It will be things I can't imagine. But if someone shares those ideas, they will land here and there. You can see the effect. People will realize they weren't the only ones with these thoughts and ideas, that common sense isn't dead after all. People who know that what they believe, who are strong within, is not what society is pushing. It can feel lonely, especially at first. But this is just an illusion. When others hear someone else express common sense in the face of madness, they respond. They say to themselves, "You know, I believe the same thing," or that sweet phrase, "You know, I never thought of it like that before, but it's the truth." So you plant a seed in the fertile ground, and you water it, and then you stand back and watch what other people can accomplish. That's how things will become better. That's how people will become involved.

Becoming an elected official is an honor and a privilege granted by the voters. I will not forget that. I will do my best to hear and speak for the voice of the majority. I will consistently defend our Constitution, including the Second Amendment. I will fight for the lives of the unborn and speak up for those who cannot speak for themselves. I will work to correct the problems in our schools while supporting the mission of our teachers. I will give our veterans the honor and respect due to them by fighting for them in the same selfless way they fought for and served us. I will support our law enforcement officers by speaking out against false narratives that condemn them, and I will see to it that they are allowed to do their job to protect us. In short, I will not forget where I have come from and the experiences that have shaped me into the man I am today.

My experience singing gives me the ability to project and phrase my speaking. I also think that watching movies, many movies throughout my life, and knowing that cinematic way of telling a story or making a point is also an important part of how I give a speech. I have a sort of inner fantasy, if you will, that if somebody gave me the opportunity, I could make a great movie, that I would strike right to the heart of the subject I was dealing with. After watching a movie I like or don't like, I sometimes sit and think about its pros and cons, what worked, and what I would have done differently.

I am a child of television and movies. But I am also a harsh critic. I can look at a film and say, "That's not what you should have done there. You should have done it this way." It is the same critical viewpoint I have when I hear others speak. I feel bad when someone is trying to make a point, but they just don't say it at the right time in the best way. I definitely critique speeches as I listen to them, just as I do movies when I watch them.

"That is *not* what you should have said there. You should have said that instead. You should have said this." I'm engaged in that moment, not thinking about ten thousand other things.

You can ask Yolanda; she knows my attitude. When I have heard a point on television or some other forum that's just wrong, I've told her I wish that I could gather the whole world together, that I could get up on a platform and tell them why that point is wrong, and what is right and why. I have convictions when I'm speaking about something, but I also have a conviction that I will find a good way to say it and to get it across. That part probably comes down to watching so much television as a kid and seeing so many examples of good and bad storytelling.

Now, in limited but important areas, I've been given the opportunity I told my wife I wanted. In addition to my wife, maybe the Lord heard my comments—and maybe it was a prayer. That is why I am so determined not to misuse this gift. I really feel that a door has been opened up by God. He did not open it up for me to abuse it, to sell it, to "build a brand," like people were trying to get me to do, to dial a number and every time somebody dialed, I'd get two dollars, or every time my video was watched, I'd get fifty cents. That's not why it happened. It happened for a deeper reason. I want to use this to inspire people.

The same with this book. I'd love to see people who grew up like me or maybe who are many years removed from growing up like me, and don't think that they're going to succeed in life to read it and say, "Hey, doggone it, I could do this too."

That's why I'm very open about some of the things I've done in my life. I have not hidden my encounters with bankruptcy and financial failure, nor brushed my failings aside. One reason is that I want to point out that financial failure is almost always the result of financial idiocy, the waste of money, waste of time, waste of opportunity, and choices that are not driven by forces outside oneself. I am no fan of NAFTA, but I, who knew better, should have planned better and avoided self-inflicted financial harm. I could say I didn't understand the system. But I didn't understand the system only because I did not sit down and take advantage of the opportunity that I had to learn the system. The opportunity to learn was there. It was open to me, as it is to everybody else.

The problem is that we let other things get in front of us. We start with what we want instead of realizing what we need. And then we start making mistakes. And once I started to understand that these issues were my own doing, I could correct the issue and turn in a different direction. That's what my wife and I have done.

A perfect example would be that first house we bought. When we got behind on our payments, we had plenty of opportunities to turn that situation around and make it right. And we *just didn't do it*. There were times when we went on vacation but should not have. There were times when we bought vehicles but should not have. Every nickel that was coming into the house should have been going toward the mortgage, toward catching up on our mortgage. You can make up a hundred excuses for why we lost the house. I didn't know the system, my parents didn't know anything about this and passed their ignorance on; I didn't understand how money works.

No.

Understanding financial systems is not closed to anybody. How to navigate those systems is not closed to anybody. I could have picked up the phone at any moment, called the bank, and said, "Give me a plan to get caught up on my mortgage," and they would have done it. They would have laid it out for me and told me step by step what I needed to do. I just didn't do it. And I could have.

That's one of my goals for young people. If you're young, I want to get you to understand: you can control your destiny. Controlling your destiny means that sometimes you must make hard choices. You may want that iPhone 15, but do you really *need* that iPhone? You might want those brand-new shoes, but do you really need those brand-new shoes? Or do you need to pay your rent? Do you need to pay your mortgage? Do you need to pay that medical bill? Don't worry about losing face. Your reputation can take the hit. Go in and make arrangements. Keep your priorities straight.

But the element of things that happen on the periphery of personal choice is also very important. For example, there was a political mistake like NAFTA, and in my case it led to Steelcase moving their furniture factory from North Carolina to Mexico. There were people around me who lost twenty or thirty years that they had put into that place; they planned on retiring there. Now they either had to start over or figure out what kind of diminished retirement they might have. It taught me the dreadful effects of a bad policy in this country—a policy that would encourage a company to snatch the rug out from under American workers like that and leave them in that position.

It's a two-way street. The government must fulfill its role. At the same time, we have to do our own due diligence. When it comes down to brass tacks, it's not what the government *enacts*; it's how I *react*. That reaction includes what I do to protect myself and what I do to protect my family. It includes whether or not I'm willing to do the right thing, the hard thing, the tough thing. That's what determines success on a personal level: the refusal to adopt a victim mentality.

We expect the government to do the tough thing, but then at home we don't want to do the tough thing, like telling the kids, "Nah, we're not going to the beach this year. We're not spending three or four thousand dollars going to the beach this year because we don't have it. We need to put that money in the bank and save it because we need that safety net in place. We'll go to the beach for two days or three days, but not two weeks. No, I'm not going to give you a thousand dollars for Christmas to spend on junk you're not going to play with after three weeks because we need to put that money in the bank and save it." Those are the hard choices we need to make at home.

Of course we have the right to expect the government to make those same hard choices in Washington, DC.

You can make all the crazy economic arguments you want, but the basic rules of financial security and sound practice don't change. Arguments that national economics are somehow different from personal economics are bogus. Economics works the same way on every level because the rules of addition and subtraction don't change. Balancing the government's checkbook is not some kind of magical ritual that changes the nature of money. The people who know this best are the ones who learn it from experience.

So many people are discouraged from running for office because they have made mistakes in their lives. They have declared bankruptcy. They have cheated on their spouse. They were in jail one time. They used to do drugs or drink. I've been looking for people who have made no mistakes. I haven't found any. Truth be told, when you go to Washington, DC, you will find people who have done even worse. There are people writing tax code who owe millions of dollars in back taxes. Look at Charles Rangel for an example. You don't get any more hypocritical than that.

So who are they to tell other people they can't run for office because of their past, that they can't do these things for their country? Do not let these people discourage you.

You and the wisdom you bring from experience and faith are exactly what this country needs.

* * *

I think back, once again, to myself as that kid living in a run-down house, sitting on the banister, pretending to fly planes, travel the world, and fight battles. I imagined myself doing so many things that, at that age and in those impoverished circumstances, I never thought would come to pass. Right now, millions of children across this nation are sitting on their own sort of banister, imagining themselves doing extraordinary things. They may be thinking, just as I did, that the role they are playing will never come true. But that is what makes this nation, the United States, such a great place to live and dream. This nation provides everyone the opportunity to chase their dreams with hard work, to speak up for what they believe, to stand on their principles, and to make for themselves the life they want.

Still, I never imagined my life taking this path. I never imagined myself becoming a household name across Greensboro, much less the state of North Carolina or the nation. I never, for one minute, thought I would be speaking at national events or having the chance to meet the famous and influential, even the president. I never could have predicted receiving an international award or having someone offer to pay me just to hear my beliefs and convictions. Yet here I am to tell the story.

How will the story end? Will I be remembered for making lasting change? For standing up for the commonsense values that made our nation great? While I hope that question will be answered with a resounding "yes," I know that ultimately God will lead me in the path ahead.

Do we shape our own destiny? Yes, in many ways we do. Each individual must determine to work hard to achieve goals and pursue the life he or she desires. I wanted to provide a good life for my family on this earth, so I was determined to work hard and teach them the values necessary for them to succeed. I did whatever it took to make a way in this world for my family.

At times, that was making pizzas.

At times, that was building furniture.

At times, that was running for office.

Did I make mistakes along the way? Yes, I did. But as I look back on my life, I realize that God has given me opportunities that I never could have created on my own. By faith, I have relied on him, and he has helped me walk through doors that I didn't even know existed. I hope I have inspired those around me, near and far, to see that it does not matter where you have come from.

It doesn't matter who your parents were, how much money you had, or what shade your skin is. God chose to place you where he did for a purpose. Don't take for granted the blessings you have right in front of you. Don't consider yourself a victim. God does not consider you a victim. He considers you his chosen conqueror, whoever you are.

And don't look around for the approval of man. Look up for the approval of God. Even if you are a failure in man's eyes, you are more than a success if God is smiling while you do his work.

He will know.

I think of Noah who was asked to build an ark. No one saw the rain coming, not even Noah, really. Everyone thought he had lost his mind. But God directed Noah, and he followed, no matter how many scoffed. So I encourage you today to place your trust in the God of creation. Hold your head up. Work hard. Pursue your dreams. And when God presents an opportunity that you may not have been looking for, don't be afraid to take it on. You never know what he is going to do with your life. As for me, I will strive to do just that.

I am an American. I am a black man. I am a Republican. I am conservative.

I am like you. I am a husband. I am a brother. I am a son.

This is the greatest nation on Earth *because* of who we are, you and I.

I am the majority.

And so are you.